Pregnant With A Vision

A Guide To Conceiving And Achieving Your Life's Purpose

LAQUINTE` BRINSON

Destiny,

& I pray this book inspires you.

LaQuinte' Brinson

ISBN: 978-0-692-10886-4

Front cover image by Richard A. Holder
Book design by RahCorp Visual Group

Hobbs Ministries Editing
LRC Editing

Printed by Create Space, Inc., in the United States of America.
First printing edition 2018.

The Break-Up, LLC
13403 Jefferson Atlanta, GA 30341

www.thebreak-up.com
CoachQ@thebreak-up.com

ACKNOWLEDGMENTS

"What you create alone is impactful, but what we create together is powerful." –LaQuinte' Brinson

I am grateful to God for trusting me to carry this vision. When my insecurities overshadowed my purpose, he still found me worthy to carry out his plans for my life. I never imagined that he could use me in this capacity, but I am so grateful that he did.

To my wonderful parents, thank you for all of the sacrifices you have made over the years to help me become the woman I am today. Your love and support carries me everywhere that I go. Thank you for blessing me with such amazing siblings that have my back no matter what. It's too many of them for me to name, but thank each of you for playing an intricate role in my process. I couldn't have asked for a better support system. I love each of you dearly.

To my dear friends that have become my family, I love and appreciate each of you. You have listened to me dreams, invested time and money and have celebrated the manifestation of my vision. I am fortunate to be surrounded by genuine people, who only want the best for me. I will never take your friendship for granted.

To my former Anatomy & Physiology professor, Renee McFarlane, thank you teaching me how to think outside the box, while embracing the concept simultaneously. Without your style of teaching I wouldn't have been inspired to write a book that bridges the gap between my love for science and my love for helping others.

To my designer Richard Holder, thank you for taking all of my ideas and bringing them to life. Collaborating with RahCorp Visual Group has helped me to take my vision to the next level.

To The Break-Up, LLC community, we have been on this journey for nearly five years and you have supported my every endeavor. There is no way that I could have accomplished what I have thus far without your support. I don't take your love and support lightly. I pray that you'll continue to be inspired by my God-given vision.

Contents

FOREWORD

Dr. E. Dewey Smith Jr.

For 30 years, I've been a veracious proponent and advocate of persons living and implementing their God-given visions. With regularity, the words of King Solomon in Proverbs 29:18, ring resoundingly in ecclesial settings, "Where there is no vision, the people perish". While an enumerable number of people have heard these words from antiquity to post-modernity, unfortunately, many have lacked a comprehensive understanding of what a vision actually looks like. A myriad of others have suffered immense frustration regarding how to ascertain and appropriate vision.

In the midst of what often seems to be impenetrable ambiguities surrounding vision, LaQuinte Brinson provides us with a refreshing illumination. With razor like precision, prodigious clarity and gut wrenching transparency, LaQuinte takes us on a journey to understanding vision. With the metaphor of pregnancy, she moves the concept of vision from the abstract and intangible to the reachable, pursuable and attainable.

For those who struggle with understanding or simply desire more insight into conceiving, casting, catching and carrying out your vision, this book is an absolute necessity. I believe and pray that this book will inform your mind and inspire your spirit. After reading "Pregnant With A Vision", my hope is that there will be a resolution to hearken to the words of Habakkuk and "Write the vision, and make it plain upon tables, that he may run that readeth it".

Dr. E. Dewey Smith Jr

Introduction

It was the summer before I was to enter my sophomore year at Riverdale High School in Georgia when I met him.

Omar Johnson, my upstairs neighbor, greeted me as I was walking down the stairs. My family and I had just relocated from Buffalo, New York, so it was good to connect with a friendly, soon-to-be schoolmate.

I had no way of knowing Omar and I would grow so close.

Everyone calls him "Big O" and because of his stocky build, and warm persona, he's the epitome of a gentle giant. That huge smile and amazing personality can light up any room, anywhere, any time. Fast forward fifteen years and my childhood friend became my adulthood confidante.

When I first launched my coaching business, The Break-Up, LLC, I told Big O about it. I wish you could have seen his face and witnessed his reaction. He was so excited, as if my vision was his own. He encouraged me to go for it and told me, "It's going to be awesome!"

That enthusiasm motivated me even more. It pushed and inspired me to keep moving forward. Truth is, Omar could have stopped there and went on his way. But he was the go-above-and-beyond type. He didn't stop there. He assisted me in tangible ways, going as far as working to connect me with other people in my field.

I was blown away by his kindness, thoughtfulness, and genuine desire to help me. Friends like that don't come along every day.

I remember the day I broke the news that I was writing my first book—the one you're currently reading. Omar was ecstatic, and just as he always has, he encouraged me.

"I can't wait to read your book," he said with that huge, signature smile, assuring me he would be among the first to purchase a copy. Unfortunately, he never had the opportunity to read it. Omar died suddenly on September 15, 2017, just three weeks after he and his wife Krystin helped me celebrate my 4th anniversary Gala of The Break-Up, LLC.

When I heard the news, it felt as if someone knocked all the wind out of me. I was sick, devastated, in disbelief. In fact, it's still tough for me to come to grips with the fact that time wasn't on my side, or his. I didn't birth my vision soon enough for him to see it come to life. Although I sometimes sit and wish I could turn back the hands of time, and be more aggressive with the process, I understand that it simply wasn't the right season.

While the loss is heartbreaking for me and all those who loved Big O, I take joy in knowing that, although he didn't live to see the finished product, he played a major role in helping shape, and build the vision. His optimism, reassurance, supportiveness, and inspiration throughout the process fueled me. His passion ignited mine. Knowing Big O couldn't wait to read it was the impetus I needed to keep working on my manuscript on days when I didn't feel like writing. I am forever grateful for him and to him. I am thankful our paths crossed and that during his too-short time here on earth, he impacted me in ways I will always cherish.

The Gentle Giant is now resting. His work is done. Mine, however, is not. Neither is yours. The fact that you are still breathing means there is more for you to do. That's why it is crucial that you are connected to good-hearted, positive, vision-building people like Big O. They fuel your passion and help you give birth to the vision inside you.

Who you associate with will directly impact your vision for better or worse, and will determine what you will create. Your relationships can be purposeful and powerful, or painful and pointless. It's up to you what kind of individuals you engraft into your life. When you consider the fact that every relationship will produce some outcome—good or bad—you will be more judicious, selective, and careful.

Just think about it; we are all a product of some form of

relationship, right? Before you were created, there was a joining together of your mother and father. Be it long-term or short-term; based on love, infatuation, or lust; a one-night stand, an accident, or incident; the fact remains, there was some form of connection or union that created you and me.

We all originated from a sperm and egg. It's the one thing each of us has in common. Whatever your race, culture, religion, lifestyle, or socioeconomic status, our origin is the same.

Even with new advancements in science, the fundamental relationship between the sperm and egg, and its essentialness for reproduction, has not changed. Without these two things, there is no creation of life.

In human reproduction, to make fertilization of the egg possible, chromosomes from both parents are joined, creating the zygote, of a new human being. Now if we metaphorically apply this reproductive example to the pursuit of vision, your purpose is the egg; your desire is the sperm. There must be a relationship between your purpose and desire for the seed within you to be fertilized, and to create something great known as vision.

Just as a woman is born with all her eggs, you are born with all your seeds of purpose inside. But it is impossible to become pregnant without sperm, or desire. If you lack drive, passion, and ambition, you will never rise to the level of greatness you could, should, or would. So what am I saying? Simply this: you have to want to fulfill your vision. Just because purpose is inbred doesn't mean it will manifest outwardly. It is your job to activate that vision by planting those seeds in the soil, tilling the ground, and creating ideal conditions for growth. Your environment can either facilitate or frustrate your birthing process. Whether birthing a child, or a new perspective, your influences matter. Tap into a toxic source and the result will be stagnation, depression, low self-esteem, lack of confidence, and all sorts of emotional issues. In light of this, you must examine your circle. Is it filled with healthy or hellish relationships? Are your confidantes motivating or hindering you? Is your core network building you up or tearing you down? Linking up with the wrong people leads to terrible consequences that have the potential to last a lifetime. Associating with the right people, on the other hand, has great benefits and rewards that propel you into destiny. Every interaction directly or indirectly impacts your vision. So ask yourself, what is this relationship creating in my life?

The importance of relationships

Whether you are trying to find your purpose, have discovered it but are struggling to get things to work, or you are working toward launching something new, Pregnant with a Vision will help you gain clarity. Whatever stage you are in on your journey toward living a purpose-filled life, this book will help you more closely examine the concepts, connections and characteristics that are necessary for giving birth. You will also be assisted in determining whether or not you are in a healthy place, and giving your vision the best chance to succeed.

I will show you how pivotal relationships are in creating and birthing a thriving vision. Even if you are laser-focused on bringing your dreams into fruition, if your associations are not in alignment with your goals, leaving those affiliations intact will be counterproductive. If you are careless with your relationship-building, you'll wind up with an inner-circle full of unambitious, inconsistent, narrow-minded, unhelpful individuals that will consequently stifle your success.

You obviously don't want that. No one consciously says, I want to sabotage my vision with dream-killing connections. And yet, their actions undermine their objectives. However well-intentioned you may be, if you refuse to move on from what no longer serves you, your best intentions will be subverted by your actions. As the saying goes, "The road to hell is paved with good intentions." And yet, it is extremely difficult to align your intentions with what you give your attention to. Truth is, operating apart from those you have grown attached to—even the unhealthiest ones—can seem impossible. But it isn't.

You must accept that some relationships expire. Some people you outgrow. I know in the beginning, pairing up with them may have resulted in something beautiful. But if that beauty has turned ugly, holding on to the past and clinging to a false ideal can destroy you. Just as well, the good thing that came out of the relationship before it went sour could be ruined if you don't put distance between you and them. Over-staying is dangerous.

Think about it. Your very first relationship took place in your mother's womb. The connection you had with her was essential for your survival and arrival. Whether the two of you are close or distant; whether she is alive or deceased; whether you agree with all her choices or not, she is still the reason why you are here. Her womb was beneficial during your growth and development as a fetus. If you would have remained inside too long it would have been hazardous to your health. Therefore, your mother had to push out—or have surgically removed—the very thing she helped create, lest her failure to do so resulted in your death.

My point? If you weren't able to stay in your mother's womb forever, what makes you think you can stay in relationships you have outgrown forever? In keeping with this idea, why would you assume your destiny can stay locked inside you perpetually, and survive? The survival of your dream is predicated upon your willingness to push it out, and release it to the world. Stagnation, or staying in the same place indefinitely, leads to death. If you want to achieve greatness, break up with your comfort. Babies have to do it.

Our very first breakup happened when we took our initial breath. The life we enjoyed inside our mother's womb ended at birth. We outgrew the environment. Our needs could no longer be supplied there. Thus, we went through a transition. Your relationships, in some cases, and your vision, will transition. You will outgrow the metaphorical womb you started in. The question then becomes, will you be courageous enough to shift before it's too late?

You won't if you allow fear to control you; it will lock you up and suffocate both you, and your vision. Fearfulness will keep you stranded on an island, too scared to drift away from shore. It will hold you hostage in a relationship with someone you have surpassed in maturity. Fear will scream, don't do it! You cannot live without this person. Mute those panicked lies. Though you may feel terrified of the unknown, launch out into the deep anyway so your dreams don't die in the womb of comfort.

This book will awaken you

Don't be lulled to sleep by complacency and meet a devastating end like the famous frog story. It goes like this: If you put a frog into a pot of boiling water, it will immediately jump out. But if you very gradually increase the heat, the amphibian won't detect the extreme temperature change because it happened slowly, and will be boiled to death. The story isn't scientifically factual, but it makes a good point. Over time, we acclimate to dysfunction and toxicity. Slowly, we adapt and settle into detrimental environments. We dwell so long in misery, we don't even notice we are wasting away.

Pregnant with a Vision is written to awaken you and remind you that your destiny is too important for indifference. Whatever you have to do, summon the strength and resolve to walk away for mediocrity, and embrace change. If you have ever left a dead-end relationship you likely felt relieved, liberated and empowered by that escape. For a moment, imagine what your life would be like had you stayed in it? It wouldn't be worth it, would it? Well, if you find yourself stuck today, it's time to dig deep once again and make your exit. There may be tears and a bit of heartache, but it's only temporary.

As isolating and difficult as the shift may be, you are not alone. There comes a time in the life of every visionary that we must release people and things in pursuit of purpose. If we don't do it, we can never release our vision to the world. Consider yourself as you make choices: are they enhancing or diminishing your vision? Is it time to break up with your symbolic womb so the world can experience the amazingness you have to offer. Contrary to popular belief, not all breakups are bad. I didn't say breakups don't feel bad. Truthfully, parting ways is critically painful, especially if you really love the person or thing you are leaving behind. However, in the long run, the benefits of saying farewell will show up.

Let me tell you a quick story before we move from the introduction into chapter one of Pregnant with a Vision. Several years ago, I noticed one of my teeth were loose. It had been wobbly for a very long time, but I never had it checked out. Finally, I got fed up with not knowing what was happening, so I made a dentist appointment. Once I was examined, I got a bit of unexpected and fascinating news.

"You still have one of your baby teeth," the dentist told me. It wasn't quite anchored like all the rest of them. As a fully grown woman, I was thinking, how in the world do you keep a baby tooth in your mouth all those years?

Normally, my dentist said, your adult teeth naturally push the baby teeth out, but not so in my case. My other teeth had actually grown abnormally around the baby tooth, which caused visible shifting and misalignment. Because the itty-bitty tooth, which had essentially over-stayed its welcome, had not been pushed out, it crowded out my other teeth. So they didn't have space to grow in properly. Before going to see a professional, I was unable to determine the source of the tooth-crowding issue in my mouth.

But a specialist instantly identified the problem. That baby tooth with weak roots was never intended to last. It served no purpose. It was simply in the way and needed to be removed. So, you know what I did? I went home and yanked it out. There was no use holding onto something purposeless that was just getting in the way of everything around it that did have a necessary function, and purpose.

Like stubborn baby teeth, there are some things and people that won't just fall out of our lives. They have to be plucked out. When we identify that they are problematic, unstable, with no depth or root, useless, and taking up space that should be reserved for our purpose, we must take action. Pluck them out. As a visionary, you will have several plucking seasons where the removal process will be necessary. Get used to that. Get comfortable with it, lest you and your vision die unfulfilled.

Before moving forward into destiny, do a personal examination. Are there people, places and things that have outlasted their season in your life? Have you hesitated to extract what is useless and simply in the way? Are you trying to dwell forever in that toxic womb of comfort at the risk of yourself and your vision? As a baby never returns to its mother's womb a second time, there are some things you have to leave and never return to again.

There are some cases where you don't need to abandon people and places altogether. But how you relate to them must change. Case and point, leaving the mother's womb does not lessen her resourcefulness to the baby. It just means the dynamics of the relationship have changed so the newborn can flourish. The infant still depends upon her postpartum, but in different ways. Whether you are forced to completely cut ties or shift the dynamics of a relationship, change, which is the only constant in life, is unavoidable. Accept it so you can go into the next phase of nourishing, guiding, and directing your life's mission. Dare to grow, improve and kick down the barriers standing between you, and your God-ordained greatness.

Moving you out of your comfort zone

Pregnant with a Vision will permanently kick you out of a cocoon of complacency, remind you that your fetus stage is over and warn you against maintaining relationships that have expired like an old container of fermented milk. Know when the season is up.

Summer does not turn to winter because you decide to wear a heavy coat. You will just end up dripping sweat beneath the blazing sun and looking foolish. You can't force an out-of-season relationship to work either by putting on a fake cloak of happiness, disguising issues, covering up pain, and pretending everything is alright. You will inevitably feel the heat and become too fatigued to keep up the charade. So why not take off the cloak and acknowledge that the season for that relationship has ended?

If you are ready to move out of your comfort zone and step into a new season of growth and success, ponder the answers to these questions. You need to be thinking along these lines as you absorb the ideas, theories, and challenges this book presents:

- What kind of relationships are essential for your vision?

- What type of relationships are detrimental to your vision?

- What are you willing to do to develop and birth the vision inside of you?

You may not have the answers to the previous questions right now, but when you complete Pregnant with a Vision, you will understand the pregnancy process of your vision. You will also know all that is necessary for you to give birth when the time is right.

Whether you are male or female, you are either pregnant with something that needs birthing, or about to conceive. Gender doesn't matter here. When it comes to vision, it is not about the joining of man and woman, or egg and sperm. Rather, it is the combining of purpose and desire that creates life-changing, and world-transforming results. If you are ready to see that seed blossom into a healthy, mature vision, keep reading. Together, we will discover powerful keys from the miracle of conception, pregnancy and childbirth, and use them as a means of unlocking your maximum potential.

Now let's get started.

1 From Potential to Purpose

Potential on its own is not enough to bring a vision to fruition.

Potential must be activated to become purposeful.

As a little girl going into the store with my mother, she would always tell me right before entering, "Now, we are about to go into this store Quinny, and I don't want you to touch anything." As far as Mom was concerned, I had no money to pay for any of the items lining the shelves, so there was no purpose in me touching them.

Never one to miss an opportunity to disobey, despite the repeated warnings, it never failed; my desire to hold and examine things always got the best of me. So I would reach out my little hand, lift things, inspect them and then—smack! I got popped for knocking stuff over and ignoring my mother's commands. There were even times when I was told that if I obeyed, behaved, and didn't touch anything, I would get a toy. I don't know what it was, but the little devil on my shoulder always whispered, Go ahead and pick it up. You know you want to.

Like clockwork, I lifted it, dropped it—smack! Repeat. I didn't get very many toys under the terms of those agreements, but I did receive plenty backhands. Now that I am older, I realize how common it is for children to have defiant streaks. Some label kids like this bad. I say they're curious. They want to know. They live to learn.

One of curious children's most frequently asked questions is, "Where do babies come from?" I love that one, because parents are left trying to find the least awkward, most amusing, and practical way of explaining this process to their child. It's always entertaining to hear the creative answers moms and dads produce in these uncomfortable scenarios. It can be a slippery slope trying to enlighten their toddlers, without exposing them to too much information that will only lead to more complex questions.

And speaking of complicated, as adults we don't lose our childlike inquisitiveness. We have wondering minds too. It's just that our queries are not nearly as simple. We ask more advanced questions like, what is my purpose? Where does vision come from? And how do I fulfill it? Unlike sheltered, wide-eyed children, who primarily rely on the wisdom of their parents, we tend to ask anyone around that seems to have found their purpose in life. We almost have a sense of desperation to know.

As a professionally trained and Certified Life Coach, I

have spoken to so many people who are intensely seeking answers related to what they were placed on this earth to do. They are waking up every day, going to work, but feeling unfulfilled in their daily responsibilities. They have this sense that they are merely existing, but are not being purposeful. They have not found out what they are here to become and accomplish. Others are frustrated because, while they have discovered their purpose, they don't know exactly how to move from theory to actually putting principles in practice that yield results.

Wherever you find yourself, throughout this book, I will be acting as the "parent," if you will, sharing clever ways to help you understand why you were placed on earth, where vision comes from, and how you can understand, and fulfill yours.

The cycle of purpose

The first thing you must know about fulfilling your vision is that it is a process. It is not something that takes place overnight, but it happens over the course of your life. The journey began the moment you entered into the world and I like to call it "the cycle of purpose."

I refer to this evolutionary process as a cycle because it is a sequence of events. It isn't one big thing that happens. It is a series of little things, one step at a time, day-by-day, year after year. You have to work at it, keep going and continue trying. You don't always become pregnant with vision on the first try. It may take a while.

Let's take a closer look at the cycle of purpose to help you gain a better understanding. As I mentioned in the introduction, every baby girl is born with all of her immature eggs. These eggs were specifically created for reproduction. Unlike men, who make sperm continuously, women are only given a certain number of eggs. Once they run out, well, that's when menopause kicks in and she ceases to menstruate. In the early stages of life, these little eggs are not very useful, but they are full of potential.

Of course, a baby can't get pregnant because the body isn't mature enough to undergo the process, but that doesn't negate the fact that the little girl is born with all the eggs that she needs to one day become pregnant. Do you see how the eggs aren't of very much service in the early stages, but are still full of potential? It isn't until the eggs have reached a certain level of maturity that the potential of the eggs evolve into purposefulness. This supports the concept that shifting from potential to purpose only happens with maturity.

Throughout the woman's life, her eggs will mature and during intercourse, those mature eggs will be released in the hopes of connecting with sperm. I want you to personalize this analogy so you understand that you were born with purpose. Notice that your potential is the starting point of your vision. You have the potential to be anything you want. However, you must go through a process of maturing that potential, so it evolves into purpose. Maturity takes place over a period of time.

You have to go through some things before your potential matures into purpose. Potential puts you in a position to create, but potential alone is not enough to create the vision. I like to think of potential as underdeveloped greatness. When something is underdeveloped, it cannot be used for its maximum purpose. Therefore, the maturity of your potential is necessary before it can be deemed purposeful. God matures you to the point where potentiality—the possibility for a thing to come into being—turns into reality. Maturation is the prerequisite to becoming pregnant with vision. Got it?

When we are born, it is within the realm of possibility for all of us to become something great. If you have not yet stepped into your greatness, don't worry. If you continue self-development efforts, over time your potential will convert to purpose. Take a moment to really think about all the potential you have and seriously consider how it can be developed into purpose. Isn't it exciting to realize that you were created with a purpose? Your potential serves as all the confirmation you need!

Embrace your cycle

Stop telling yourself that there isn't purpose for your life. Don't spend another moment entertaining that asinine conversation in your head that questions whether or not you are a mistake, or if your life has any value. You are purposeful. Your existence has meaning and you were born with everything you need to produce greatness. Stop looking around you to find your purpose; instead look within in you. You don't have to waste another day wondering if you have purpose. Work on developing your potential and your purpose will show up when you are ready.

Know this: Everyone reaches maturity at different stages in life. Therefore, your cycle of purpose may not move at the same rate of speed as others'. But that doesn't mean you are behind, nor does it discount the fact that you were born with purpose. When you become overly consumed with another person's process and timetable, you begin discrediting your own. Your path won't always resemble the path of someone else, but that does not denote that you're on the wrong track. Your process is uniquely tailored for your vision.

Maybe someone else did it younger, faster, or what you perceive to be better than what you did. That is the wrong mindset. Embrace your cycle, your evolution, and your journey that is required for your potential to mature into purpose. No two paths are alike. You cannot compare the timing of your process to those around you. It's so easy to get caught up in where someone else is. If you aren't careful, you will find yourself wanting something that you don't fully understand. There is always a part of someone else's story that you don't have access to. You don't know what they did, how they suffered to get where they are, or even if what they appear to be is actually genuine.

Shift your focus to what it will take to fulfill your vision. You haven't missed your opportunity. You're not too old. It's not too late for you. Every life experience is bringing you closer to destiny. Those life-shifting events worked to mature you and increase your chances of becoming pregnant with vision. The relationship that didn't work out; the job you lost; the rejection you faced; the degree you earned and couldn't find a job for; the trauma you endured; the loved one you lost; yes, all of those things have brought you a step closer to becoming pregnant with vision.

Until you actually birth the vision, you may not see the worth or relevance of the hardships. This is why enduring the process is a must. You will never appreciate what you went through if you quit before you have the chance to actually come through it. Each of these happenings is significant. They are positioning and preparing you for your purpose and your desires to collide to form vision. Without these occurrences, you wouldn't be ready to conceive or achieve anything. I know it may be taking longer than you expected. You might have asked yourself, why don't I already know what I was placed on this earth to do? But you must trust that time will reveal exactly what you are meant to be and do.

The wait is working for you

In January 2016, I got really ill and was hospitalized. Initially, I thought I had a persistent virus of some sort causing the high fever, vomiting, and other disturbing symptoms. But after my head felt like it would explode and I could no longer manage the pain, I sought medical attention, and it was a good thing I did.

My blood pressure was through the roof and doctors couldn't lower it, so they admitted me. At its highest, my pressure shot up to 276/124. My eyes were bloodshot. My body went through all different kinds of changes. At moments, I felt like I was going to die. I was fatigued, weak from being unable to keep anything down, and deeply concerned. Through tears, aches and rough nights, I prayed that God would help.

It was an up-and-down process. My parents flew into Atlanta to be at my bedside. Friends came to see about me and helped take care of me. Because I am very independent, being dependent on others was very uncomfortable. I wanted this whole saga to be over. All I could think about was going home to my quiet apartment, getting back into the swing of life, and putting this whole ordeal behind me.

Though I wanted to hurry the process along, there were certain things my medical team wanted to see regulate before they would let me go. If I didn't reach specific markers and wasn't showing any promising signs, they held me right there. Though I had to stay hospitalized longer than I wanted to, looking back on it, I needed to be where I was. I had to go through the process. Had I been discharged too early, the consequences could have been fatal. Premature release leads not only to physical death, but to the death of vision, which is why waiting is a good thing. It also happens to be one of our least favorite things to do.

When it comes to the conception of purpose, get used to waiting, because things aren't going to happen prematurely. Take female eggs for example. As she develops, so do her eggs. Understand that it takes years before the eggs are mature enough to be purposeful. Maturity is gradual. It takes time. Rushing the maturation process ultimately leads to premature pursuit of purpose—and a whole lot of vexation, and frustration.

There is no need to whiz through the process. Time is the most precious gift, but also one of the most unappreciated. At some point, we have all wished we had more time. I know I have. When you feel like you have insufficient time to reach a goal, you become overwhelmingly agitated. But the great thing about time is that, even while you're moaning about needing more of it, time is still being used to develop you for your future.

Through frustrating seasons, it doesn't stop preparing you. The wait does its job of preventing the premature entrance of an immature you through a door, onto a platform, or into a relationship you don't have the character to sustain. If given the chance in your immaturity, you would unwittingly destroy your chances of being purposeful.

The wait is working for you. So don't waste time being frustrated over time. Instead, maximize the time you have. Let it develop your potential and mature you for your purpose. To reiterate, don't spend precious moments complaining about time. Every moment spent complaining is another moment lost preparing. How many valuable seconds, minutes, days, weeks, months, or years have you lost murmuring and grumbling? Potential must be strengthened and developed before it can be fruitful. So if you're still questioning if there is a purpose for your life, let me answer you with an emphatic absolutely! Having potential is having unrealized purpose; it will eventually be realized with maturation.

Even what you don't understand is necessary

The fact that you're still reading Pregnant with a Vision indicates that you have not been put off by the fact that you will have to wait. There is a hunger inside of you for destiny. You want to conceive. Even with knowledge of the basic fundamentals of conception, which includes an extended— and sometimes frustrating— period of waiting, you are yet interested. That's a good sign.

Since I have your attention and you are bent on pursuing purpose, I'm sure you want to know, what is necessary for maturity? That's an important question for which I have the answer. Maturing is a process that requires three things: growth, development and detachment. All three are essential for the maturing of your potential. Now, in the reproductive process, potential isn't limited to eggs. In fact, there are specific events all throughout the cycle that must happen in order for potential to reach the correct level of maturity, and then activate into purpose.

That last statement is pretty abstract and a lot to digest, so let me give you a great scientific example of potential being activated into purpose. Each month, a woman's Follicle-stimulating Hormones (FSH) are released. The FSH hormone is responsible for producing what is known as the estrogen hormone. Estrogen is needed during the conception process, because estrogen causes the uterus to thicken. Why is this important? Here's why.

After a woman conceives, within days, the embryo implants into her uterine lining, also known as her endometrium. When the uterus, where the embryo resides, is nice and thick, it provides a safe environment for the fertilized egg. If it were not for FSH and estrogen, the uterus would be too thin and weak. It wouldn't be able to provide enough support for that egg. Therefore, it would be unsafe and the pregnancy process could abruptly end, leading to a miscarriage. That's pretty fascinating, right?

Though this is a scientific concept, open up your mind a little more so you can understand its direct parallel to your life. You see, it's easy to dismiss the importance and usefulness of follicle-stimulating hormones and estrogen hormones if you don't understand the purpose they serve, and how profoundly they impact pregnancy. We tend to be dismissive of things we don't see, both literally and figuratively. But even if you had never heard of these hormones and didn't know their functions, that wouldn't make them any less necessary for conception.

Similarly, we can't see the purpose of every life event. We don't understand how every single thing is working together for our benefit. We don't like dealing with puzzling or painful circumstances, but these are the very things that thicken our skin and toughen us up enough to carry the vision, so we won't miscarry. Be resolved to respect all of the process, even the parts you cannot see or grasp. Know that their necessity is not negated by your lack of understanding.

You must realize that every component of your process has a unique and necessary function. Everything you have endured up to this point was maturing you so your vision would not stop at conception. Once that embryo or seed implanted itself in your uterine lining or your heart, those skin-thickening agents like trouble, transition, and trauma, were ensuring that you were built to successfully give birth.

The hormone concept supports the idea that when you release your potential, you activate your purpose. Let's examine this more closely. Estrogen is released before the egg ever connects with the sperm. Think about that for a minute. This hormone doesn't wait for the woman to get pregnant to start working. Even when there is no apparent need for the uterus to thicken, the estrogen hormone does its job anyway. It sets things in order so when the time is right, and the sperm fertilizes the egg, the woman's body is prepared to carry the seed to maturity.

In the reproduction process, potential is at work before purpose is revealed. Nothing visible may be happening as it relates to your vision, but the cycle has already begun. In the fullness of time, potential and purpose will collide. You may be facing rejection today, but you still have a purpose. When things are taking longer than you expected, you still have a purpose. It hasn't manifested yet, but you still have a purpose.

It's up to you, however, to release your potential so that you will discover your purpose. What are you waiting for? If estrogen refused to release in the name of waiting for the egg

and the sperm to come together, the uterus wouldn't be ready for pregnancy. So how do you expect to be prepared for the pregnancy of your vision if you're not releasing your potential on a consistent basis? Those who wait and see, will always wait, and never see.

Don't delay the activation of your purpose because you procrastinated on releasing your potential. If you don't own a business, be a good employee. If you haven't started your own nonprofit yet, volunteer for other community service-oriented organizations. If you haven't written a book, start journaling. If you want to be a great leader, be a great servant. All these things will mature your potential into purpose. Stop waiting on a sign before you start doing something.

It is important that you understand that potential isn't useless; it's just immature. It can still be effective at laying the foundational groundwork for your future purpose. View potential like a muscle. It becomes bigger and stronger the more you utilize it. Eventually potential will take shape and morph into exactly what it is intended to be—that is, if you work it.

Are you beginning to see how potential works—that once it is mature, it activates your purpose? To be clear, potential alone isn't enough to create something great. If it is untapped, it does nothing. Potential has to first be active before it can be activated into purpose. Stop holding onto great ideas and letting them lie dormant in your mind. Release them into the universe so they can be activated. Get busy.

Breaking up is good

We have already talked about two of the three things necessary for maturation: growth and development. But we cannot leave out detachment. Releasing your potential requires you to detach or disconnect from some people and things. It is a breakup process. The word "breakup" has such a negative connotation, because it denotes the end of a thing, but it really can be something positive. As it relates to the cycle of reproduction, breaking up is a sign of maturity. We leave the womb when we are capable of thriving in a new environment.

Have you ever felt compelled to leave your womb of comfort to create a healthy environment for your vision? How did it start for you? Did you sense the need for transition before supporting evidence showed up? Did you feel the urgency to get things in order? On previous occasions, I have sensed the need for a shift, without any recognizable signs of confirmation. In the past, I ignored that inner-knowing, because I told myself I was over-thinking or overreacting. Whenever I hesitated, eventually, the proof that the shift was necessary showed up.

That's why I say, if you know you need to break up, do it. Take measures to clean up your environment for the sake of growing your vision. There won't always be physical indicators serving as signs. Nevertheless, it is better to trust your spirit. What you sense won't always be validated by what you see. Carefully weigh your current decisions by the impact they will have on your future. Vision requires sacrifice. Releasing people, habits, behaviors, and emotions is essential before any of us can create the ideal atmosphere for vision to thrive.

Breaking up is another thing that has the estrogen hormone effect on us. It thickens our skin and makes us strong enough to do what is necessary to carry our vision to full term. If you hold on to things longer than you should, you will stay at the same level with only recycled strength. But when you release hindrances, you discover renewed strength. You can accomplish even more, take on greater challenges, and handle more responsibility.

For that to happen, separation is necessary. Everyone and everything can't be around you when you're in the process of becoming pregnant with vision. Let go of what you no longer need so you can create an environment that will support your growing vision.

Take a few moments to examine your life. What must you release so that you can place yourself in a position to become pregnant? What is making your environment weak and unstable? Whatever it is, it's purging time. Get rid of the clutter. Set the stage. Stop trying to create a new set with the old props. Your purpose is waiting on your potential to mature, and your vision is waiting for you to activate your purpose.

You can become the greatest inhibitor to your vision when you're not willing to turn things loose. Letting go signifies you are ready for something greater. What are you willing to give up to move closer to conception?

Just as our body sends a signal to release a specific hormone to set processes in motion, the signals in our lives tell us when it's time to break up. Sometimes we overlook those signs, as I have done, because we just aren't ready to move forward. But hesitating prolongs your process. The longer you take to detach, the more time will take to become pregnant with vision.

Purpose Ovulation

Aren't you tired of getting up every day and feeling unfulfilled? Aren't you sick of living vicariously through the social media filters of others? If you make sacrifices, you won't have to live your life through a filter. Detach before you destroy your chances of becoming something great.

Here is another scientific example of breaking up that will show you why it is necessary to let things go to produce something greater. As the egg matures, the body receives a message to release another hormone known as luteinizing hormone (LH). The release of LH is what triggers the body to release mature eggs. This process is known as ovulation. During ovulation, the woman's chances of becoming pregnant are significantly increased. That's why some women who want to conceive take ovulation tests. These predictor kits identify the woman's fertile window, helping her discover the best time to engage in intercourse to improve the likelihood of her conceiving.

At the ovulation stage, potential has now matured into purpose, so the chances of being pregnant are very likely. You will know when your purpose is ovulating because new doors will open, giving you access to new places, where you can form the right connections. Things begin to click when you're ovulating. During this part of the cycle, the mature egg makes its way to the uterus and waits on the sperm. If no conception occurs, the uterine lining that went through a process of thickening when the estrogen was released, will then go through a shedding process. The uterus will thin out and the egg that never connected with the sperm will also shed, which is what triggers menstruation. To all my men reading this book, you now understand what happens during the menstrual cycle. Basically, the woman's body was prepared to become pregnant, but the eggs didn't collide with the sperm. Therefore, she didn't conceive. If, on the other hand, the woman doesn't have a menstrual cycle, this is usually an indication that the egg and the sperm have joined together to create a baby.

The way the process unfolds is fascinating, and yet, many will never see, know, understand, or appreciate the significance of how the individual parts all work together to achieve the goal of conception. It is at this very stage that we understand why hormones needed to be released, because what they released, which was not visible to the eye, is what made the pregnancy possible. This is what I call "purpose ovulation."

Purpose ovulation is the stage at which your potential has matured enough to be purposeful and evolve into vision. Just as the body must release a mature egg to wait on the sperm, you must release your gifts and talents, and move purposefully on a consistent basis. During this phase, you are on the brink of conception. Your purpose is waiting for just the right time to be activated, like the mature egg waits on the sperm. Your purpose is waiting on your desires, your passion, and your action.

God has wonderful things in store for your life, but how bad do you want it? Are your desires strong enough to move you to act? If your passions don't push you to do something, you will simply remain passionate without producing anything. You will be reduced to a talking head, always discussing, vision casting, meeting, brainstorming, gabbing away about what you want to do, but won't ever do it. Knowing what you have been purposed to do isn't enough; you must have the desire, the will and the discipline to fulfill it. When you want something bad enough you will motivate yourself to go after it.

It is true that your purpose will prepare you, but your desires will position you when your actions are in alignment. Like the egg and sperm, your purpose needs to be connected to the right people, and things. It is imperative that your environment caters to your vision. Your atmosphere can either drain you or inspire you. When you plant your vision in the wrong soil it can't be used for its intended purpose. It will either be abused, neglected, or misdirected. In a healthy environment, you will bloom. When you surround yourself with like-minded individuals it keeps you on track. But when you are tied up with people lacking goals, aspirations, and focus, you end up either frustrated or off course. I know companionship provides certain comforts. We all crave it. But prioritizing temporary satisfaction over long-term success, sets you up for failure. Your passion for purpose must be greatest of all, because you will need all the inspiration you can muster.

As you're reading, you may be wondering, What about when I have been doing everything right, but I still haven't gotten pregnant? There is no need to be discouraged; there is still time. Prepare while you wait. Make some changes to increase your chances of becoming pregnant. You may experience difficulties along the way, and it may even feel like it will never happen, but it will. You just have to stay true to your process. Don't waver in your pursuit when your outcomes aren't in alignment with your goals. Don't allow temporary defeat to deter you from reaching your destination.

Perhaps you thought it would have happened by now. You may have smiled and celebrated everyone else's pregnancy while wondering, when will it be my time and my turn? Don't get distracted looking at everyone else around you; stay committed to your process. You may even have to go through the cycle a few times before you become pregnant. That's very common. Don't allow yourself to become overly-frustrated with the wait. Choose faith over frustration! Everyone doesn't get pregnant on the first try. Does that mean they should stop trying? Absolutely not. It only means that it isn't time yet. Have you considered that God is still developing you?

Instead of being discouraged by the success of someone else's vision, allow it to inspire you to keep working towards achieving yours. Your road to conception may be a tad more complex, requiring greater effort than the average person. You may run into obstacles while trying to get pregnant, and hear one negative report after another. But keep working toward it. Don't pass up new opportunities because of past opposition. There will be other chances. You just have to be in the right place at the right time, which is why mindfulness about where you spend your time, and who you spend it with, is crucial.

Do you recall what I shared about relationships at the beginning of Pregnant with a Vision? I talked about the power of relationships and how they either bring you closer to your vision, or separate you from it. It is wise to be selective about the company you keep and the locations you frequent. Every interaction is an opportunity to activate purpose and become pregnant with vision.

Why?

I will never forget the day I was sexually assaulted by a classmate in my senior year of college. I was so angry. I didn't understand how something that devastating could happen to me. I was deeply confused and felt a great deal of betrayal from an individual, whom, before that moment, I regarded as a friend.

I remember how terrified I was by his actions. I was utterly shocked and disgusted at the same time. I was depressed for weeks. I was immobilized by grief. It was like I was in a haze and could not chase the sorrow away. I didn't want anyone to know what he did. So I was imprisoned by this secret. Some days, I couldn't get out of bed. I was trapped in a pit of despair.

Why? I couldn't reconcile it. It tortured me night and day. For years I held on to the agony and let it fester inside until it grew toxic. Angry, bitter, and scorned, I wasn't any good for anyone—including myself. The residue of what happened lingered. It got so bad, I became more loyal to my pain than my purpose. I neglected my vision. With all the time it took for me to deal with what transpired, I thought I would have been able to gain some sort of clarity or perspective.

Sometimes, it takes years to gain an understanding of

why you endured something horrific. There are certain instances when you will never understand. Some things are senseless. The why won't ever become clear, and yet, that doesn't mean that incident, however hurtful, can't fuel your purpose. I believe everything you go through is a prerequisite to fulfill your unique destiny.

Back when I was first sexually assaulted, if you had asked me what that had to do with my vision, I could not have told you. But today, I have a different outlook. Because of that painful experience, in all its ugliness, I am now able to empathize with the pain of other sexual assault survivors and those experiencing deep levels of pain. The magnitude of trauma increased my capacity to understand and assist the broken, depressed, hopeless, and lost. I wouldn't be as effective in my purpose today without that anguish. Although the experience was awful, by the grace of God, I went through a process of healing and can now help others heal.

Though God doesn't cause them, He uses our painful experiences to activate our purpose. Nothing you've been through is useless. Don't be disheartened over the complexity of your life. You might not have been through sexual assault, or maybe you have. You could be simply wondering why you've gone through so much in your life in general; why you've cried so many tears; why you've been isolated and never fit in with the crowd; why you were rejected so much;

or why nothing ever seems to work out for you.

Being matured for purpose doesn't feel good. It feels like punishment, but God isn't punishing you. On the contrary, He's preparing you. He understands what it will take for you to birth your vision and wants to make sure you can withstand the process. He has given you something of great value, and hardships, like estrogen hormones, make you stronger and more resilient. Trials give you the tools you need to protect your vision and avoid miscarriage. The things that hurt you the worst taught you the most, too.

I've been through many other difficulties in my life. I couldn't figure out how they all worked together until I tapped into my purpose. When I saw how even the most painful things were purposeful, and served my vision well, I drew peace and comfort from that.

Moments of frustration

We all love getting to the part we understand and things make sense. We like it when we get our equilibrium back and feel balanced, and whole. But before things click and come together, there will inevitably be moments of frustration. This is why I enjoy helping you see purpose through the lens of a metaphorical pregnancy process. It is a highly effective way of illustrating that birthing your vision can be quite the rollercoaster ride. Throughout the book I will continually remind you that every part of your process is necessary for the fulfillment of your vision.

In the introduction, I referred to the egg as purpose and sperm as your desire, and the two come together to formulate the vision. Once the egg is released, it leaves the ovary and enters the fallopian tube. If all goes right, it is here that the egg and sperm come together, and demonstrate the power of connections and interactions. The sperm is just as significant as the egg, and is equally necessary to create the vision. The male organs are always creating sperm. During sexual intercourse, when the man reaches the point of ejaculation, millions of sperm are released. They must travel through the uterus and up the fallopian tubes before connecting with the egg.

Many of the sperm will die during this process; only a small percentage will reach the site of the egg. In most cases, only one sperm out of millions can penetrate the egg. If the sperm successfully connects with the egg, then what? That's where babies come from, or, for our purposes, that's where vision comes from! However, if the egg never connects with the sperm, or the sperm never reaches the egg, fertilization won't take place. Shedding occurs and as a result, the menstrual cycle will begin, and the process must start all over again.

This shedding process mimics moments of frustration:

those times when you do everything by the book, but the outcome doesn't render the results you hoped they would. These occasions can be extremely vexing when you are working to become pregnant with vision. Though our desire for vision survives these disappointments, we may question our purpose and feel unsure of whether we even know what it is anymore. Trouble has a way of making you question everything you thought you knew about yourself, your life, and your dreams.

But lack of certainty doesn't mean lack of purpose. In times like these, don't stop doing what you know is right and believing that soon, your fertile season will manifest. Sometimes, we have all of the components in place, but the timing isn't right. Keep on waiting. Learning to trust God's timing and His plan will help you as you move into the next phase.

Before you continue on to chapter two, make sure your faith is strong. Be confident that your day will arrive to become pregnant with your vision. Everyone has a different story. Some plan it and it happens quickly. Someone else doesn't plan at all, and it happens unexpectedly. Others need multiple attempts. Whichever story is yours and whatever the circumstances, the truth remains: it will happen.

2 Congratulations! You're pregnant

Even if you feel unprepared to carry the seed growing inside you, know that everything you need to be successful is inside of you.

"Can you hear me now?" I asked for the umpteenth time during a phone call I placed to one of my sisters from Buffalo, New York.

On that December day, I was starting to feel like the "test man" character from those old Verizon Wireless television ads that debuted around 2002, and lasted for nine years before dropping off. Do you remember them? The guy with the horn-rimmed glasses would travel to the most remote locations and ask the person on the other end of the line, "Can you hear me now?" Then he would follow up with a one-word answer: "Good"—signifying that the invisible respondent said *yes*, they could hear him.

The commercials framed Verizon as a reliable service provider that enabled customers to effectively communicate with no frustrating connection issues. This was a clever marketing ploy that engendered consumer loyalty and wooed others in search of a dependable communications network.

Whenever I talk to my sibling, she laughs and teases me about my service provider that shall remain nameless. I must admit, though, a lot of calls *do* drop during our engaging conversations, particularly when I'm on the move. That afternoon, I happened to be in a part of town where the reception was especially terrible. More than half the time, she couldn't make out what I was saying, which isn't the norm. Typically, if my phone drops a call in one spot, it's an easy fix. I just move to another location—sometimes, only a few inches away and everything regulates. But not that day. I couldn't find the right conditions to preserve our connection. It was no use. We finally decided to hang up and stop talking.

It didn't matter how badly she and I both wanted to continue speaking, laughing and exchanging information. Without connection, the desire alone was not enough to turn what we hoped for into reality. Here's my point. We each have desires. Depending on what they are, our passion to see them come to life can be very intense. But if that intense desire is not connected with persistent action in pursuit of purpose, nothing will happen. We'll just be passionate and unproductive. Our heads will be filled with big dreams, but our lives will be empty and devoid of purpose.

If you want to accomplish something, you cannot afford to drop the connection between your desires and purpose. You are your own service provider. You are the carrier of your vision. You can't point the finger at anyone else and say *my call dropped, my dreams died, my vision never succeeded because of you.* We are hardwired to place blame in the face of failure. It is human nature to pass the buck, but it is also crippling and debilitating. If you are serious about conceiving and achieving your life's purpose, take complete ownership of your actions, and stop at nothing to marry your desires with your purpose. When you do this, you will be unstoppable and nothing will be impossible for you.

The power of connections

"What we create alone is impactful, but what we create together is powerful." –Coach Q.

There will be some connections you make in life that are as essential for fertilizing your vision, just like a sperm's connection with an egg. Once this fusing together is complete, the fertilized egg immediately begins undergoing change. These changes prompt new connections in the woman's body that are important for growth and development. A cycle of transformation starts.

Once your purpose and desire merge, and fertilize into vision, you will see a metamorphosis. New relationships will formulate that will ultimately help grow and develop your vision even more. Key connects will set off a chain reaction and get things moving in the right direction. This happens when you enter the "germinal stage," which scientists describe as the first stage of pregnancy. In this phase, the zygote—the female egg that has been fertilized by the male sperm and can now grow into a fully developed baby—once positioned for proper growth.

Zygote comes from a Greek word meaning "to join" or "to yoke." What you are joined or yoked to matters greatly when it comes to vision. Are you connected to the right people? Are you in the proper position to be fruitful and productive?

Notice that the first thing that occurs in the germinal stage is placement. Positioning is critical as the zygote is preparing for the full-term pregnancy process. *Your* vision in its germinal stage also needs to be in the correct position to grow and develop into its full potential. Have you been wondering what's going on with your ideas, business ventures, books, songs, movies, inventions, and other not-yet-realized goals? They are incubating and being prepared for the series of events ahead. Let this analogy motivate you to get in position to grow your vision. Don't be in your own way and become the reason you're in a place of discontentment.

You can't see it, but something is happening

During this stage, it's important to note that there is no detection of your vision. Yet, that does not rule out the fact that you are indeed a vision carrier. It is inside of you. It's just imperceptible to the senses right now. There isn't always evidence of the seed implanted within. But in due time, as the seed grows, it will be visible to all. Don't give up prematurely. The seed must first grow underground before it can manifest over-ground.

If you allow frustration to govern your actions, you will give up before you reap the benefits of what you have already endured. Think about what you had to go through just to get to *this* point; why would you throw it all away because of what you can't see now? Nothing you have survived is in vain. It is all relevant: every tear, disappointment and loss was necessary to set you on the path to destiny.

Perhaps, now, you readily acknowledge that life experiences, good and bad, prepared you for your divine purpose. But while you're in the middle of uncomfortable seasons, you may be unable to figure it out and see the value or significance in the setbacks, and struggles. Initially, you might feel like, *why me, God?* During the germinal stage, when what has been deposited in you remains intangible, you have no choice but to trust the process. Believe that it won't be like this always. You will bring forth something greater at the appointed time.

Let me point out that some scientists argue that during the germinal stage, the woman is not actually pregnant yet. Those who adopt this view believe the body is just *preparing* for pregnancy. This is a hotly debated theory. Whatever side you fall on, it cannot be denied that the body *is* preparing. Preparation is an indication that something is getting ready to take place. Although there may be no outside detection, there is something inside signaling the woman's body to adjust to a new reality.

Do you sense that you need to get ready for something greater? Don't ignore it. It's an indicator that you are on the verge. At this period in your life, you may only possess components of your vision without having the *actual vision* itself. For example, you could be a gifted writer without a book. The fact that you have not yet published your work does not mean you never will. You have at least one of the essential *elements* required to be a best-selling author. Don't ever discount your elements because you haven't figured out how the puzzle fits together.

Work on your manuscript. Do your homework by researching what it takes to be an author. Focus on the fact that you have the basic, essential components to create the vision, and don't get discouraged. If you stay on track, it is only a matter of time before your vision blossoms. As long as the foundation is there, you can be confident that the process will yield the desired result.

Check Your Environment

If you, like the zygote, find a healthy environment, you'll be well on your way. But you must be wise and understand that your vision will not grow and thrive in just *any* place. Makes sure your surroundings are well-suited to your plans before you embark upon the vision. A seed planted in the wrong environment can be damaged or even destroyed before it has the opportunity to grow, and thrive. You must find a safe place to cultivate and mature the vision.

We have established that the attachment of the fertilized egg is an essential component of the process before an embryo can form. You will develop attachments in your life, too, that are critical to the embryonic stage of your vision. This is why the habitat of the seed you are carrying is important; your vision will attach itself to your environment, for better or worse. If you believe your vision is unaffected by your locale, you're putting your life's purpose at great risk.

Let me break it down. Once the embryo is properly attached to the uterine lining, pregnancy can be confirmed—not before. The attachment causes the production of a very important hormone known as "human chorionic gonadotropin," more commonly referred to as hCG. Once hCG is released into the bloodstream, a test can be taken to confirm pregnancy. Your vision cannot be detected until you are in the proper place. Do you realize your environment could be what's preventing you from recognizing that you are pregnant with vision? If you remain in a space with dream-killers, negative people, critics, and those who don't see greatness in you, that will be problematic. That's why, sometimes, you have to relocate before you can discover what is inside of you.

Now, once you're in the right place, it doesn't stop there. The only way to confirm that there is really a vision growing, is to be tested. I know no one likes tests, trials, and hardships, but visionaries don't get to skip them.

When I Became Pregnant With Vision

Becoming pregnant with vision wasn't something I planned, nor was it something I initially wanted. However, through the process, I have learned to love my vision. Now I can't imagine life without it. It has introduced me to a new world. I never knew I could feel so fulfilled. Living out your purpose gives you such a sense of gratification that is nearly impossible to describe. I had no idea birthing my dream was the puzzle piece I was desperately searching for my entire life. I had no clue I was equipped to carry something so great. At first, it felt like a burden and not a blessing. I wanted to get rid of it. Today, I'm thankful I endured the process.

When I became pregnant with *The Break-Up, LLC*, I felt like a woman who feels ill-equipped for an unplanned, surprise pregnancy. I was confused about how it happened, because I used protection. I didn't just go around activating my potential. I was careful and focused. I didn't understand how something like this could happen. I was also nervous, because I didn't think I was fit to carry the vision. The thought of birthing it was even more terrifying. I wasn't ready.

How did I let this happen to me? Who would support me? What would everyone think of me? I was in a very selfish state of mind and I didn't want anything to separate me from my plans—not even my purpose. Yes, you read that right… not even my purpose. As an expecting mother that views her pregnancy as nothing more than an accident and a disruption, I was upset. I was so wrapped up in my personal goals, I assumed they were synonymous with God's. So you can imagine, once my potential matured into purpose, and I got pregnant with a totally different vision than I expected, I was completely shocked.

I remember when it happened so vividly. I was sitting at my desk at work on a Friday afternoon. I was patiently waiting for five o'clock to come and greet me so I could head home, and enjoy my weekend. I was minding my own business, not looking to engage in any extracurricular activities. However, before that time could arrive, I heard the word *breakup*. It was *so clear*, it immediately grabbed my attention. I just sat there, stunned, allowing nothing to distract me.

The longer I sat, the more I heard. Not only did I hear, but I also began to envision everything I heard. The message was simultaneously profound and invasive. I knew it was God speaking to me about developing my purpose into a life-changing vision. This was, for me, the *purpose ovulation* stage. My potential had matured and it was released. The environment was just right. No one was around and nothing was breaking my focus. I ended up grabbing a sheet of paper and a pen, and jotting everything down. I let my guard down. I couldn't resist and I took in every word I heard.

As I began to do so, tears streamed down my cheeks. Still, I kept writing until I could no longer see through the tears that were profusely pouring from my eyes. When I finished transcribing what God was downloading and showing me, I sat there sobbing. I knew that conception of my vision had taken place. There was nothing I could do to reverse what just happened. Although I hadn't yet taken my vision pregnancy test, I knew I was pregnant.

My vision was in the germinal phase. There was no physical detection, but the Spirit of God confirmed it for me. I continued to weep, realizing what had taken place. I wasn't crying tears of joy, however. They were tears of confusion, disappointment, fear and anxiety. At this time, my potential had developed into purpose. My desire to become something great penetrated my purpose and my vision was fertilized.

But again, I wasn't happy about it. I even considered aborting my vision so my life wouldn't be interrupted by this unplanned seed. I didn't want to receive judgment when I sprang the news on everyone that I was expecting. I didn't wish to hear the opinions of others. After all, I had invested several years and money into my education to be a doctor. This detour didn't fit the script. I didn't think I was cut out for it. I wasn't open to this kind of life shift. The crazy thing about being pregnant is that, you don't have to feel like you're ready, you just have to place yourself in the position to get pregnant. I had gone through all the necessary steps to get pregnant, but I didn't want to *be* pregnant.

Too bad. It was too late by then. My potential matured; my purpose was released; my desires activated my purpose; and before I knew it, I was pregnant with vision. My unplanned pregnancy felt like a major inconvenience. I didn't understand how I could be pregnant with my own organization when it wasn't what I studied for in college. I was always cautious about the books I read and the classes I took. But somehow, I still became pregnant with my own organization.

When God Disrupts Your Plans

My entire life, I had dreams of practicing medicine, so I felt like I was protecting myself from becoming anything else. I went to college, studied biology, went to grad school, and studied public health. And I still ended up pregnant with an organization? Huh? How could this be? I mean, sure, I have always known that I had the potential to connect with people. But that didn't mean I believed I could, or even wanted to do it in the way my vision required. God disrupted my plans.

My desire to become great and touch the lives of everyone I met was overwhelming, and it penetrated my purpose. I worked extremely hard to make sure my story ended with greatness. I just didn't know the magnitude of the seed that was planted inside of me. Just like the natural process of reproduction, the sex of the embryo cannot be manipulated and neither could my fertilized vision. I was pregnant with *The Break-Up, LLC* and there was absolutely nothing I could do to change that.

Even after knowing I was expecting, I went through a phase of neglect and denial. I somehow allowed myself to foolishly believe that my lack of attention would magically cause my unborn vision to vanish. As a result of my poor logic, I did not tell anyone the news. I continued living my life as if there was nothing different. I didn't switch up one thing about my routine. I made a conscious decision to stay in denial, but I couldn't ignore the reality. I was pregnant. My usual thought process was interrupted because I could only seem to focus on my pregnancy.

While trying to pretend the symptoms of being pregnant with vision didn't exist, I knew I needed to nourish my vision. As the days and weeks went on, I began to notice changes. My spirit became more sensitive to God. This changed my mood, thoughts, interests and interactions with people. I started hearing God's voice more vividly. I had to silence my thoughts of self-doubt and the overwhelming feeling of inadequacy, and solely depend on what God instructed me to do.

I finally remember waking up one Saturday morning with a scripture on my mind: Habakkuk 2:2. Oddly, I had this verse in my head, but I didn't know what it said. So I grabbed my smart phone. I like to think of it as my vision pregnancy test. I went to my Bible app and began reading Habakkuk 2:2. It said, "Write the vision and make it plain..." In that very moment, with confirmation from the word of God, I tested positive.

After receiving spiritual evidence of my growing vision, I went through a phase of self-doubt. Truthfully, I allowed it to dominate the beginning of my process. That lack of confidence kept me from enjoying the early stages. I had no faith in myself, which prevented me from believing that my vision was purposeful. Once I released the feeling of self-doubt and focused more on my faith, I learned something: before I could trust the process or myself, I had to trust *God* first. I knew I had to embrace the truth, even when I was afraid and felt inadequate.

I had to rid myself of the thought that God had given a perfect vision to the wrong carrier. I made a decision to trust Him. I believed He would guide me. I started reminding myself that the process would prepare me for the birth. Although fear of the unknown hung like a shadow over my head, the love for my unborn vision illuminated the path forward, and motivated me to push past fear. I had to become more faithful to the process than I was fearful of it.

It wasn't easy to redirect my loyalty from fulfillment of my personal plans to the fulfillment of my purpose. Fear never stopped showing up, but neither did my faith. I found myself growing along with my vision. And my faith got stronger every step of the way. There were times when I was afraid and I second-guessed myself. But I kept going until I birthed my vision.

The rollercoaster of emotions

It's always interesting to hear the responses of expectant parents. Whether you ask the mother or father how they feel, the reactions are unique. You will find that there are a plethora of emotions that accompany news that a baby is on the way. Some are happy, sad, excited, afraid, anxious, embarrassed, panicked, and the list goes on. Rarely is there just one emotion. It's more like a rollercoaster of highs and lows as the new reality sets in.

There is no right or wrong way to feel initially; the newness of the experience awakens all sorts of feelings. Depending upon your personal circumstances, the revelation will cause you to ask a series of questions like, *am I ready for this? Who will support me? Can I do this? What is everyone else going to think? Is it normal to feel overwhelmed? Should I be more excited? What am I going to do?* This is especially true if it's your first time. Even if it's not, pregnancy will make you ponder all sorts of things. Ultimately, the process changes you and you'll never be the same.

Some emotions last throughout the entire pregnancy; others come and go. But whatever feelings the life-changing occurrence evokes, you must not allow negative emotions to take away from the beauty of your process. I understand that not all circumstances are alike. Some pregnancies are not planned or even wanted. Nevertheless, there is a beautiful blessing growing inside. It doesn't matter if the pregnancy was on purpose or not, it still is a gift. The greatest blessings can sometimes come from the most painful situations. Keep in mind, being pregnant with vision doesn't require the perfect conditions or the perfect person. You just have to activate your potential and allow your purpose, and your desires, to come together.

Who said being pregnant with vision was a fairytale?

When marketers produce pregnancy ads, they give us warm and fuzzy feelings. There's a smiling expectant mom, so excited about the bundle of joy she's about to bring into the world. In advertisements, there only seems to be love, light and happiness surrounding the glowing mom-to-be. Not only that, but many times, when we hear others share their packaged, sanitized versions of becoming pregnant with vision, it can seem like things fell into place overnight. We often hear trite sayings like, "One thing led to another and the rest is history."

Perhaps your story of becoming pregnant with vision didn't go like that and didn't resemble anything close to a fairytale. This makes me think of my friend Danielle Allen, whose story I featured at my 3rd Annual Gala. She and I attended Riverdale High School together. We also attended the same college, Albany State University. To look at Danielle, who is an exceptional educator for Clayton County Public schools, committed to helping children be great, you would not imagine the heartbreak she has been through. On her 21st birthday, her pregnancy was confirmed, which she said was scared. But that wasn't all. Danielle was informed that the baby would be born with cerebral palsy.

"It definitely hurt my heart to know that she would suffer," said Danielle in a recorded interview with *The Break-Up*. She was admittedly very sad when her baby girl, whom she named Taylor, was not well enough to come home for the first month after entering into the world. Her beautiful daughter was diagnosed with Epilepsy and Cerebral Palsy. So, as Taylor grew, she was unable to stand, sit up alone, or feed herself.

One night, Taylor got very ill and Danielle took her to the emergency room. While there, the doctors were able to get her fever down and sent her home with Danielle. "Once we got home, the only thing that was wrong is that she just kept crying," explains Danielle. "I couldn't understand why she kept crying, or what was wrong with her. She would be dried. She would be fed. So I would keep going to her room and checking on her."

The last time Danielle went in to check on Taylor, she says, "It was like I was in a movie. Her eyes were open and she was just cold. I just ran to the phone and called 9-1-1." Over the phone she was given instructions on how to perform CPR on her little girl. She did the best she could. Then the paramedics and a police officer arrived. A valiant effort was made to resuscitate sweet Taylor, but eventually, Danielle says, "They came outside to tell me that she was gone."

I remember being with Danielle at the funeral and witnessing the pain and devastation that I could do nothing to ease. She loved Taylor so much and was forced to say goodbye. After that heart-wrenching loss, Danielle was depressed. She didn't want to get out of bed. She drank to numb the pain. At her lowest, she began mixing alcohol, antidepressants and pain pills—something she acknowledges was "dangerous." Twice, feeling unable to cope, she tried taking her own life, but thank God, my dear friend is still here. Over time, by the grace of God, she began finding her way. Still, she takes it one day at a time.

Though the gut-wrenching loss of Taylor took Danielle to a very low place, her story of strength, courage, and the will to live in the face of tragedy, is inspiring others. She bravely shared her testimony at the Breakup Gala in 2016 where I was so happy to honor her. Opening up was another important step toward healing for Danielle, and an encouragement to others to keep on going. As rough as the road was, do you see how the tragedy helped activate her purpose? Back when she was numbing her pain and mourning the worst moment of her life, she never knew God could use something that ripped her to shreds to mend others who are devastated and broken-hearted, too.

Danielle's story reveals that even tragedy can be a part of purpose. Something resulting from a painful situation truly *can be* a blessing. But let me be honest. The reality is, you *won't* always see the good in every life event right away. But you must trust that all things will work together for your good. Don't be discouraged by what you see in the beginning, because you can never know the full story without going through the process.

Clearly, perfect conditions aren't a prerequisite for vision; therefore, it's not by mistake that you have been chosen to carry and soon birth this amazing dream. Stop giving so much attention to the imperfections of your circumstances (or yourself for that matter!), and learn to be grateful for being divinely chosen to carry such a significant gift. If you're not careful, you will talk yourself out of birthing your vision. It may not seem like it, but you are more than capable of fulfilling your purpose that God has destined for your life. In this process, use positive thoughts and affirmations to get you through. Don't dare doubt your ability to give birth to what you have been called to do; activate your faith.

Don't ignore your vision

Perhaps your story of being pregnant with vision is different from mine and Danielle's. But the fact remains, your purpose and your desires have come together to develop into vision. Don't ignore your vision. Embrace it. Acknowledge that there is a special treasure growing within and causing you to change. You're no longer the person you used to be and you can't just live life for you anymore.

Consider the seed you're carrying. At the conception stage, even though you may not see it, every day, tell yourself this: *I was born with purpose and my desire to become something great has now fertilized into a vision. It's up to me to fulfill the process of birthing my vision.* You are strong enough to endure the growing pains, sleepless nights, physical, mental, and emotional changes built into the journey. Have faith in your ability. If you don't, you may opt to abort or ignore what's inside. Unfortunately, if you decide to terminate the pregnancy, you'll never find out how wonderful your vision could have been. You won't get to see how it might have transformed your life and the lives of others in positive ways.

I implore you not to ignore this invaluable treasure. Trust the process and put your faith in God. He is the One who selected you to carry this gift. He has planted something special in you. Not only did He put it there, but He will also assist you during every stage and phase on the journey toward birthing your amazing vision!

3 Before Your Vision Is Visible

The intangible seed in the early stages cannot be seen, but if you water it with faith, it will grow.

The first trimester, which lasts for approximately thirteen weeks, is believed to be the most crucial stage of development. So much takes place. Cells are rapidly growing and developing, and coming together to create a healthy embryo. Right now there is only a teeny seed, but it's still so valuable. The value of something is not determined by measurements; your vision doesn't have to be big for it to be valuable. Do you ever wonder how something so itty-bitty becomes something vast? The answer is growth potential.

Remember at the beginning of the book we established that potential is what matures into purpose? Your vision is just like a wee embryo; it starts off as a small seed, full of potential. You can't see it, but invisibility doesn't mean it is valueless. Believe in your vision, despite its small beginnings. Don't allow the initial size to cause you to discredit the magnitude of its greatness. The size of the seed doesn't compare to all that will come from it. Find pride in carrying your little seed of greatness. No need to become insecure at the start. If you knew all it would become, you would be extremely proud. Just keep on feeding it so it can bloom into what you desire.

At this point, your pregnancy has been confirmed, but the seed, your vision, seems miniscule. You can't see it. But for visionaries, seeing isn't believing. In the words of my good friend Greg Kirkland, "people don't believe *because* they see it. They believe *until* they see it." Know that you are on your way somewhere great. Though it will take a while to get there, approximately 40 weeks, take this into consideration: it isn't nearly as long as an elephant's pregnancy. Did you know that elephants have the longest gestation period of all mammals? They carry their seed for around two years, about 95 weeks, averaging 680 days.

That's a *long* time. Once they enter the world, after such a lengthy period, elephants, known to be highly intelligent, have had sufficient brain development in the womb. At birth, they are capable of functioning effectively in their environment. On average, an elephant calf is born weighing about 265 pounds. No wonder it takes so long for them to develop in the womb! God always takes His time on greatness.

When we are pregnant with vision, we cannot predict how long it will take, but we can be sure that each day we wait is necessary. God is up to something incredible, so don't get in a hurry. Prematurely giving birth to a child or a vision can be detrimental. Full development is essential to the health and maturity of the seed. That's why the wait is worth it. Whether you feel like it or not, you have what it takes, for as long as it takes, to carry the vision from conception to birth. You have been given the responsibility to nurture and care for the greatness budding internally, because you can handle it.

It sounds like a pretty big responsibility, I know. And it is. Still, there is no need to worry. The newness of the process can be a little intimidating and it's okay to feel somewhat anxious. But even with the feelings of uncertainty, I am confident that you've got this in the bag. Your entire life has prepared you for this experience. Everything you have endured was necessary for the process ahead. You must trust that you're strong enough to get through anything that comes along with your pregnancy. Self-doubt is toxic, so believe in your vision and your capacity to carry it. Trust that God has given the *perfect vision* to the *perfect person*. That doesn't mean *you're* perfect, but you are perfectly suited for your purpose.

Think positively, because it will add peace to your process. Eliminate any negative conversations going on in your head regarding what you can't do and what may go wrong. Remind yourself that you are not in this process alone. God is with you every step of the way. Tell yourself, *I am capable and I will get through the process of birthing my vision.* The conversations you have with yourself can provide all the motivation you need. Or, they can discourage you, making you believe you can't carry your vision full-term. Your thoughts have power over your actions. Choose positive thoughts and positive actions will follow. Focus on building your confidence until you fully believe that you are ready. The fact that you are chosen proves that you are.

Have faith

It was my sophomore year of college when my dad drove my 1994 Chevy Cavalier all the way from Buffalo, New York to Albany, Georgia. My cousin Nia had given it to me after she received her new car. I was so excited about having my very first whip. The only downfall was, well, I didn't know how to drive. I had a permit, but no license, and I had only been behind the wheel a few times.

My driving skills were far from impressive—*very* limited, in fact. I remember my dad giving me a pep talk, letting me know he had put me on his insurance policy, but didn't want me driving until I got my license. I replied, "Yes sir," assuring him I would do as he requested. Then, one afternoon, my roommates and I made plans to hang out later. It sounded like a great idea, so it was all set. We headed to campus that evening to have dinner in the cafeteria.

On the way there, we had the windows rolled down and I was cruising behind the wheel of my '94 Cavalier, with no AC, in ninety-degree weather! We were living our *best* lives in that sweltering heat. My roommates and I safely arrived on campus. Everything was going smoothly ... until I tried to park. As I was attempting to navigate my way into a space, one of my friends, seated in the back, got scared because she thought I was going to hit one of the cars next to me. Little did I know, her fear was about to become reality.

She yelled out, "Quinte'!" I panicked and hit the gas instead of the break. Instead of crashing into one car, I actually plowed into about four vehicles, dragging one of them out of the parking spot. I completely totaled the Cavalier. No one was injured, but my ego nearly died that day. I was *so* embarrassed. I called my dad crying frantically, letting him know I had wrecked the car. Obviously, I wasn't ready to drive and had no business disobeying Dad's orders.

Aren't you thankful that, when God impregnates us with vision, He knows we have the capacity to handle the assignment? He won't put us in the driver's seat of destiny prematurely. He sets us up for success by only giving us a vehicle to release our purpose once He has licensed us to drive. If you think you're not strong enough, wise enough, or equipped enough, think again. Not only do you come fully loaded, but over time, as your vision demands greater capacity, God will increase you in every way. While God was maturing your potential into purpose, He was also strengthening you to carry your vision. Have faith.

I know it's so common to hear about faith and trusting the process. Further, I am aware that it can be tough. However, faith is essential for the journey. Doubt and fear will make things harder than they need to be. But unflinching belief will allow you to embrace the changes, sacrifices and the pain. At this stage in a natural pregnancy, you won't be able to see the internal growth of the baby, but you'll need to have faith that everything is growing properly. Faith is what allows you to see beyond your circumstances. Faith will remind you of what you're capable of when you feel like you can't. Faith will become a way of life as you commit to the process of birthing your vision.

While having faith is extremely beneficial, you must also be sure that your actions are in alignment with your faith. If you believe that you will birth a successful vision, rid yourself of unhealthy habits, so your vision can reach its full potential. Its survival is dependent upon your lifestyle. Your conduct should be in compliance with what you're expecting to give birth to. If your expectation is to have a successful pregnancy, then you must operate in a manner that leads to success. Let your actions be on par with your goals.

Protect and nourish your vision

You are no longer just living for yourself. Your vision, though not yet visible, is thriving. It is also totally dependent on *you* for survival. Consider all the seed will become and all the lives that will be positively impacted by it. Your vision is depending on you for protection. The delicacy of this first trimester requires that you create barriers. Prevent harmful substances and people from coming into contact with your vision. Don't allow anyone or anything to jeopardize its survival. If you don't protect what you're carrying, then who will? It is your responsibility to watch over your precious cargo.

Your vision is relying on you for nourishment. What are you feeding it? In the natural pregnancy process, the mother feeds the baby through the umbilical cord. Everything she ingests has a direct

LAQUINTE` BRINSON

impact on her unborn fetus. Your vision can only *ingest* what you *digest*. Tailoring your diet is necessary. That means you have to make sacrifices. Some things you really enjoy may have to be totally removed from your regimen. You'll need to reevaluate your diet.

Put faith in place of fear; confidence in place of comparison; and determination in place of doubt. What you feed your vision is a reflection of your lifestyle. You can't lead a negative existence and expect to feed your vision positivity. Being pregnant with vision will challenge you to make life-altering changes. Build yourself up. Load up on encouragement, motivation, scriptures, positive affirmations and anything else that fuels your greatness. You can't feed your vision anything that you don't have. Therefore, activating your faith and adjusting your lifestyle will both serve as assets to your developing seed of purpose. What you do during this stage plays a massive role in determining whether or not you'll birth a healthy vision at the appropriate time.

Greatness in a small seed

During the first three months, your vision is tiny. It's difficult to see physical growth. It is comfortably contained in your womb and not many people will recognize the greatness growing there. Although the seed in beginning stages may not be visible to those around you, you still have a responsibility to care for it.

While in this phase, you won't be stretched too far. In the not-so-distant future, however, the demands on you will increase. You

66

will look retrospectively and appreciate the first trimester. But don't let that stress you. Your capacity becomes greater with time. As your vision grows, so will your ability to carry it. The first trimester doesn't render much physical evidence of growth, but you can rest assured that it *is* growing.

Consider the bamboo tree. When bamboo seeds are planted, they are planted several feet apart so that they have room to grow. The distance between the seeds lets me know that the expectation of the one planting the seed is high. Even still, with bamboo seeds, there may be no physical evidence of growth until the fifth year, depending on the species, and environmental factors. However, just because there is no growth *above* ground doesn't mean there isn't any growth *underground.*

The growth that is occurring below ground ensures the roots will be strong enough to support the size of the tree that will eventually shoot up above ground. For several years, there is no sign that an enormous bamboo tree will soon sprout out of the dirt when the time is right. But the sprouting will only occur if the seed is provided with proper nourishment. During the extended period without physical evidence, careful attention must be given to the seed to meet its requirements for sunlight and water.

Can you imagine watering a seed for years, but seeing no growth? Perhaps you know *exactly* what it feels like and may be discouraged by that. I know how that feels as well. There are some things in my life that I am still watering and I don't see the physical manifestation. But my expectation hasn't changed. Year after year of watering the same spot and witnessing no change can be a bit of a let-down, but you must not give up.

What happens if the planter stops nurturing the seed? It will never grow and reach its full potential. Therefore, the role of the planter doesn't change just because there is no physical evidence of growth. Your role as the visionary is to be consistent in times when consistency yields nothing and seems useless. The first trimester is like this. It is very similar to the first four years of growing a bamboo tree. Despite no indication of flourishing of your vision, it is your duty to take care of the vision God has entrusted to you. Let your expectation of giving birth in due season motivate you to nurture the seed in the meantime.

Being persistent when no growth indicators are visible is the mark of a true visionary. As is the case in human pregnancy, there are several weeks when your vision is undetectable. No matter how many pregnancy tests you take, they all come back negative. Why? Because it's too early to tell. Pregnancy hormones show up in the blood around week four. Not until then will you test positive, and be able to validate the process that had already begun, without confirmation.

When the outside doesn't match the inside

At the outset, you won't appear to be pregnant, but the changes inside will soon reveal that you *are* pregnant with vision. You will notice transformations first before anyone else does. You will become more sensitive to your spirit and your surroundings as a result of what's growing inwardly.

What's manifesting on the inside is impacting how you behave on the outside, even if there is no outwardly visible change. As it relates to this stage of vision, you may live in the same house, drive the same car, frequent the same job, live in the same city, have the same network, and are at the same income level, but something is brewing. There is a higher calling, a deeper purpose, a sense of passion, and an awareness of a greater mission you are called to fulfill. When the outside doesn't match the inside, this leads to frustration for some. But hang in there. You'll show some signs of growth after a while.

Even before what's inside shows up on the outside, embrace the truth that you are, in fact, changing. Go ahead and make modifications in your lifestyle at this early stage. Making tangible changes on account of an intangible seed, to some, seems ridiculous, absurd and premature. It isn't! Your vision *always* starts off as something intangible, but the pregnancy process is what allows it to become tangible. Do things to foster growth like: spending more time at home instead of going out; saving money for your vision instead of going on a shopping spree with friends; or planning a "staycation" instead of a vacation to conserve resources. These are all changes you can make at this stage. Others might not get it, but that doesn't matter. Make the most of this time. Preparation is critical. Let your present actions align with your future expectations. When in doubt, assure yourself that something powerful is growing that is worth the sacrifice. You can't see it or touch it right now, but don't allow your inability to naturally see and touch your vision, make you believe it isn't there.

During the beginning weeks, those around you won't likely know you're expecting unless you tell them. The seed is hidden deep inside. In the beginning, a woman's stomach doesn't change much, though rapid growth is happening inwardly. The expectant mother, who isn't yet showing, doesn't receive the preferential treatment of someone who is in the advanced stages of pregnancy.

The few-weeks-pregnant woman won't be handled with the same level of care as a woman whose belly has popped out. In the first trimester, an expectant mom will stand for an extended period before being offered a seat. She may be the last one to eat, even though she's eating for two. She could easily be mistaken for having a nasty attitude, although she's experiencing mood shifts due to hormonal imbalances. Misunderstanding dominates this phase. There are some people who will judge you only by what they can see.

Unfortunately, they won't always treat you like you're pregnant with vision. But don't allow the way others handle you to be the standard for how you handle yourself. Even if they don't acknowledge or cater to you like you're pregnant, that doesn't invalidate you or the reality that you are expecting. It is up to you to set the standard for your vision. Let them dismiss you, as long as *you* take the initiative to care for your vision. With persistence and time, it will grow to the point that it can't be ignored. As you treat your vision well, soon, others will, too.

When the outside doesn't match the inside, don't expect recognition, praise, or even encouragement. You are more likely to get pessimistic responses, confused looks and criticism. Don't sweat it. Others not perceiving your greatness does not cancel it out. Their mistreatment or misperception of you cannot stop the growth and flourishment of your vision.

Give yourself a daily reminder that your vision is great, powerful, and totally worth the investment. When you're mishandled, mistreated and mistaken for insignificant, if you're not careful, the mischaracterization will get you off course. Don't let it. Dust your shoulders off. Keep doing what is best for your growing vision. Your responsibilities are too great for you to let anyone defeat you mentally and dictate how you view *your* journey.

If necessary, change your circle. Everyone can't be a part of your process because they don't understand the magnitude of what you are carrying. Letting them fall by the wayside is one of the best things you'll ever do for yourself and your vision. You have to be around those who respect you as a person, as well as the purpose you are called to, even *before* they see signs that you are pregnant with vision. Anybody can celebrate you once you step into destiny. The ones who are true, that will remain in your life for the long haul will celebrate, motivate and see the value of what you're carrying, long before it sprouts up like the bamboo tree.

The signs and symptoms of pregnancy will eventually come. When they do, you don't want bandwagon-hoppers that just want a free ride. You need authentic individuals that stood by you before the outside matched the inside, and rooted for you before your greatness was visible to the rest of the world.

Uncomfortable symptoms are normal

As your pregnancy continues to advance, you will become more symptomatic. Symptoms, that cause moments of discomfort, vary for each individual. One of the most common first trimester issues is morning sickness. It is the body's response to a variety of hormones being released into the bloodstream all at once. It usually takes a while for the expectant mother to adjust to the hormone influx. For many women, morning sickness lasts the entire first trimester.

Initially, you feel overwhelmed with metaphorical morning sickness. The side effect is frustration. At this stage, you get easily agitated as a visionary. You are a bundle of raw emotion as your anticipation grows, but nothing else seems to. You are ready to get on with things and see something happen. When you don't, it sickens you. The delay can be maddening.

Just as in the natural, a woman's stomach isn't yet poking out, but she's sick. With your vision, much hasn't changed in your life, but you feel altogether different. This is irritating and disruptive to your daily routine, but it won't last forever. The disruption of your comfort zone is a sure sign that your vision is growing.

The morning sickness associated with your vision will mess up your usual everyday practices. You will be forced into making adjustments. You may suddenly want to change career paths, take a huge leap of faith, or attempt something no one in your family, or your circle of friends, has ever done. Your appetite may switch altogether and things that once satisfied you, won't anymore.

Vision will separate you from what's familiar and from things you love, and enjoy. Don't lament this shift. See separation as a growth stimulant. Throughout my process, I've learned that it is nearly impossible to hold onto all the things and people you are attached to, and still cater to the needs of your vision. I have had to make *huge* sacrifices. I've shed some tears, but it was worth it. What was familiar brought me the most comfort, but it was stifling my growth.

Choosing my vision over my comfort didn't initially feel good, but it has paid off in many ways already, and will continue to. The way I see it is, my level of sacrifice is in direct proportion to my vision's level of greatness. To whom much is given, much is required. Ask yourself, *is what's familiar worth neglecting the needs of my vision?* If you can't honestly answer yes to that, isn't it about time you made some changes?

Believe in your vision

Remember I told you I crashed my car one night on campus? Well, after going months without a vehicle and being taken me off of my dad's insurance policy, I was left without a car and *still* no license. Though some things had changed for the better since my embarrassing fender bender, the no car thing was a major inconvenience.

I had moved off campus into a nice apartment with my friends. That was cool, but it was tough getting to and from school. I was at the mercy of the drivers' schedules. I had to leave early in the morning to get to campus and leave super late to get back home. I was bothered by that. I was tired of relying on others to transport me to and from school, and work.

So, one day, I decided I was going to change things by getting another car on my own. Mind you, I knew nothing about financing a vehicle, but I decided it was time. After diligently searching, at first, I was told *no* because I didn't have enough credit. I also was informed that I didn't make sufficient money from waiting tables. A college kid bussing tables for a living, with pretty much no credit history, wasn't appealing to banks. But somehow, I got approved by the dealership anyway.

They asked me to come and test drive the new car. Learning from my last experience, I was a bit wiser. I asked my roommate to test drive it for me. All went well. That same day, we drove off the lot with my new 2004 Chevy Cavalier. And yes, this one had AC! I phoned my parents and told them I bought a new car. They were both confused and excited at the same time. Before purchasing it, I had not informed them of my intent to do so. I knew they would have tried to talk me out of it. In their minds, I didn't need a car at the time. I mean, what for? I couldn't drive, so why would I take out a loan for a new automobile? To avoid hearing that kind of lecture, I kept my plans to myself. They didn't know the level of stress I was under, or how much I would be helped by having transportation of my own.

After becoming a vehicle owner, I knew I had to get my license. I quit procrastinating. I got behind that wheel and did what I had to do. The more I drove, the better I became at it. Once I felt confident, I scheduled my road test. The morning of, I was a ball of enthusiasm and frantic nervousness. I buckled myself in and drove around the streets of Albany as carefully as possible. After about 20 minutes, I got the best news. I successfully passed my driving test on the first try and was issued my license. Sometimes, your process won't make sense to others. But you have to trust yourself and go for it, even if it seems illogical to those around you.

As it relates to your vision, wouldn't it be wonderful if everyone believed in it right away, before they saw the fruit of it? Wouldn't it be outstanding if they trusted your decision-making rather than looking at you with an eye of skepticism? Sure, that we be incredible, but we know the world doesn't work that way. Don't expect special commendation right off the bat. Believe in yourself. Pat your own self on the back. That has to be enough.

As I've already stated, in the first trimester, the way you look won't correspond to the way you feel. Moments when you're not treated like you're pregnant are moments where you learn the significance of your responsibility. If you *were* initially treated like what you're carrying, you would need special treatment going forward. Whatever it took to get you there is what it'll take to keep you there. If you had to have heavy doses of validation, hand-holding, coddling and spoon-feeding to make it to the top, you'll require the same thing to secure your spot long-term. When you believe in your vision, whether people are cheering or jeering, it won't make a difference.

Know your worth

People's devaluation of your gifts and talents doesn't change that you are invaluable—which means all-important and irreplaceable. Your greatness is not for everyone to see initially, because some would try to sabotage it before you birthed it. That's why God will allow the treasure within to be hidden until its full maturation. That way, it can survive what is intended to destroy it.

Don't get aggravated when others don't know your worth. It is of paramount importance that your valuation of your gifting and calling be weightier in your mind than someone else's evaluation of it. How do *you* see what you're preparing to give birth to? What is your vision like in your estimation? That's what counts. In its embryonic stage, it is yet a gift from God. Treat it that way.

I am reminded of a time when I was among a group of people planning for a singles conference. They were asking for support because it was a new endeavor. I went up to the leader of the group and offered my services. I told him I had been affiliated with similar events. He looked at me and said, "You can't speak at the conference, but you *can* speak behind the scenes of the conference." I was utterly confused by that reply. He then went on to say I could participate in the meetings leading up to the event. He encouraged me to offer my opinions and ideas to those that *would* be speaking. However, he made it clear that I would not be permitted to address conference attendees.

Initially, I was upset and outdone. My feelings were hurt. After all, I was pregnant with this great vision and I understood the magnitude of it. But he didn't. He disregarded my capabilities because I didn't have a big name or major platform. He was dismissive of my vision in the embryonic stage. Now I know he simply needed physical evidence of my growth before he trusted my vision. He didn't do anything wrong. His response was equivalent to the way most people treat first-trimester-visionaries. No matter how amazing their vision is, without visibility, most will not honor, respect, or value it.

Although the experience was painful, I didn't let it stop me from nurturing my seed. I used that experience to motivate me. I pulled myself together and said, *it is up to me to take care of my vision and to develop my own platform to help it grow.* I knew that one day the value of what I possessed would show. Even a diamond doesn't look spectacular at first. It goes through a process to reveal its brilliance.

Before it ever makes it into the hands of a diamond cutter with the skill to bring out its beauty, in its rough state, it is still valuable. The same is true about your vision. Before it is refined, it is valuable. Before it is fully defined, God knows its brilliance. Don't wait for someone to assign value to what is yours. Know your worth.

While the embryonic stage of pregnancy is not usually detectable to the average person, there are a select few that don't need the visible characteristics to know that you're pregnant. I remember hearing the older women in my family saying, "I dreamed about fish, so that means someone is pregnant." For instance, your mother may be able to recognize the fullness in your face before the roundness of your belly appears. When individuals can detect the pregnancy minus the signs, it is a blend of their experience as a visionary and their connection to you. Visionaries don't have to see the full picture, nor do they need to know all of the details to spot the divine purpose growing inside you. They will support the changes you make and encourage huge leaps of faith.

They will treat you like you're already walking in manifestation. They will plan, prepare and pray with you, until your vision is birthed.

They try to assist however they can to alleviate the stress and negative symptoms they know so well. They won't judge you harshly when you make changes that seem premature to everyone else. They will play a significant role in the birthing process. You need them, because no one can birth their vision alone. Be grateful for them. They have been strategically placed in your life by God to help you.

Form before function

In the first trimester, the organs begin to develop as embryonic stem cells multiply. In the course of the first thirteen weeks, the nervous system—the brain, spinal cord and nerves—form. But immediate function does not follow the formation of vital parts of the nervous system. Just because something has formed doesn't mean it is functional. You must give it time to develop, before expecting it to operate the way it will in its mature state.

The heart forms, but doesn't immediately beat. The facial features form: eyes, ears, nose and mouth. Yet, the anatomy of the face is not coupled with sensory function. The arms and legs form with small ridges that eventually develop into fingers and toes, but the mobility of the embryo is not yet voluntary. Lastly, sexual organs begin to develop. However, the sex of the embryo cannot yet be detected through an ultrasound. All of the major components of the embryo begin to develop but without complete function.

The core of your vision will begin to develop in the first trimester. Processes will take shape, but they won't be operational. The foundation will be there. Much like a building with nothing more than a foundation, the groundwork of your vision has already been laid. Now you have something to build upon. And God, the Master Architect, who created the blueprint, has the times and seasons for the completion of the edifice under His full control. But building is a process.

At this stage, as a visionary, you will start to see components that are needed, but they won't operate at the outset. No need to get vexed. Be patient. When the fullness of time comes, things will flow and work together. Growth cannot be rushed or manipulated. If someone is striving to advance more quickly, this can lead to premature functioning, resulting in unnecessary complications.

Let the process take its course. Be okay with starting small. Zechariah 4:10 says don't despise small beginnings. The vitality of your vision is developed in the initial stages. Trying to skip steps results in an underdeveloped, dysfunctional vision. Development takes a while and there will be components that don't initially seem useful. But they will work eventually. As you eagerly await progress, don't diminish your vision in its infancy. Don't allow the wait to discourage you. Learn how to appreciate who you are and what you have now, on your way to where you're going.

The first trimester forces you to get comfortable with uncertainty. You don't have to know where every puzzle piece goes before you begin putting it together. Work with what you have. As you continue to use what's already in your possession, you will acquire more. You will not be given everything at once; it will come in stages. It would be great to have it all right away. But if you did, it would take away from the significance of your process.

Before we move on to chapter four, let's recap. The first trimester demonstrates that the beginning stages of your vision equip you for the entire process. Just because you don't see anything happening, does not mean you are stagnant. Seeing is not believing. We are limited by what we physically perceive; we are limitless when we are guided by what we believe.

So then, increase your expectation. Anticipate growth. Over time, you'll begin to see the significance of every part of your journey. Pay attention to how everything is formulating from the inside out. There are things that must develop internally before manifesting externally. It's called a vision because you *see* it in your mentality before you *possess* it in reality Don't disregard your vision during this stage, because without it, your foundation would not develop.

4 Embrace the discomfort

Being a visionary isn't easy. At this stage, you will be required to stretch, abandon your comfort zone, and adapt to change as you prepare to give birth.

I waited tables at Longhorn Steakhouse for five years. The income got me through college. I didn't like my job, but it was the most convenient means of making money while attending school full-time. I made pretty good tips, so that was the trade-off. It worked for me.

That's why I broke down when, in July 2010, just two months after graduating, I lost my position. It was devastating. When this negative life shift transpired, I was living in Atlanta alone, preparing to apply to medical school. Suddenly, the comfortable, though imperfect, life I'd grown used to, changed. I was living off of unemployment, making only $231 weekly. That wasn't enough to cover my bills. I didn't know *what* I was going to do.

I wish I could say that, shortly after, I found a new job. But I didn't. I went fifteen long months with no work. It was during this time that I ventured into entrepreneurship. I tutored kids in math, which brought in much-needed extra bucks. Somehow, by God's grace, I was able to pay my bills and never miss a beat. That doesn't mean it was easy. Difficulties arose. I thought I would have to move to Buffalo with my parents. But in the nick of time, I landed another—much greater—opportunity.

Before things turned around, I was confused and frustrated. I was blind to all the ways the process was developing me for where I am today. Years removed from it, I now have clarity. That introduction to entrepreneurship was necessary. The inconvenient season showed me that tough moments will arise. But I have to push through, keep going and know things will get better. Life teaches powerful lessons.

It has taught you as well. What you have learned has equipped you for your second trimester. By now, you are no stranger to persevering through hard times. Because you stuck with it, your vision is growing and thriving. You're closer than you've ever been to giving birth. You didn't allow your feelings of inadequacy or uncertainty to make you abort. You didn't let emotions overwhelm you, thereby robbing you of future success. You managed to get through one of the most difficult stages of pregnancy. That's a big deal!

What a powerful way to enter into your second trimester, knowing that nothing you were up against was able to separate you from your dream. Allow the strength gained from what you've already endured to motivate you to keep progressing. Although there is a significant amount of time left before you actually give birth, it is still important to celebrate how far you've come. In the past, I was guilty of focusing too much on the end result and forgetting to acknowledge small milestones along the way. I had to learn how to enjoy the ride and be patient. The process has purpose.

Can you imagine if you birthed your vision immediately, without a gradual progression? There's no way you would be ready. As you reach new benchmarks, be sure to reflect on how you got started. Look back on your history. Doing that can serve as the greatest motivation. Retrospective glances and reflections will prevent you from giving up prematurely. When you see and acknowledge what you have survived, you'll be reminded that you have the grit to dig your heels in and thrive despite challenges.

The fear factor

You may feel a sense of relief now that you have made it through the most delicate stage of your pregnancy. You, like many women, may have waited until you completed your first trimester before broadcasting the news. While conducting research for *Pregnant with Vision*, I asked a few mothers why they waited until at least three months had gone by to tell everyone they were expecting. I noticed that one answer was more common than any other. The majority of moms said they were afraid to tell everyone, when they knew there was a possibility that the baby wouldn't survive. According to The American Pregnancy Association (APA), 10-25% of all pregnancies will end in miscarriage, and most miscarriages happen within the first 13 weeks. So, most women spend their entire first trimester excited, but also quite fearful.

Once I learned that the fear factor caused most of the women to privatize what was going on in their wombs at the start of their pregnancies, I dug deeper. I asked each of them, "Was your fear of losing the baby greater than your faith that you would give birth?" The question seemed to catch them off guard. It also proved revelatory for them, in that, it made them see they held more tightly to fear than faith.

However reluctantly, each mom agreed they had unknowingly been loyal to their fear of losing the baby, rather than celebrating their blessing in faith. There is such a powerful lesson to be gained from the honesty of these expecting mothers. You don't have to be a biological mom to understand this analogy. Consider the times in your life where *you* gave more attention to your fears than you did to your faith. I've had plenty of them. When I first became pregnant with my vision, the fear factor was real. I didn't tell anyone for months because I was afraid of feeling inadequate. Fear can become a very dominating emotion if you allow it to be. Left unchecked, it will rise up and choke out your faith.

If you have been controlled by the fear factor, ask yourself, *why have I made fear my companion in this process?* It should really be the other way around. Cater to your faith and abandon your fears. Take faith with you wherever you go. Fear will cause you to keep your vision private, but faith allows you to bless others with that God-given dream. I've learned that your vision doesn't have to be fully developed before it serves as a resource, and asset, to you and others.

When I first launched *The Break-Up, LLC,* I didn't have my business license, my logo, or a website. All I had was the seed that God planted within me to help individuals break unhealthy life cycles and become the very best versions of themselves. Your seed can be a blessing before it produces fruit if you pair it with the right things. Coupling my seed with faith, inspired others to do the same. If, on the other hand, you plant your seed in the soil of fear, others that you are called to lead by example, will follow your lead, and abort their seed. Originally, I gave too much power to my fears, but eventually, I broke up with them and began to boldly operate in confidence.

I launched my vision with a social media post that said, "I'm going through a breakup." That was my second trimester pronouncement that I was expecting. And from that moment on, I've been giving more power to my belief than my doubts. Trusting God liberated and empowered me to announce my pregnancy. Are you trusting God the way you should be? He will help you when your vision isn't robust if you tap into faith. When your vision is undeveloped, you don't know where the resources are coming from, so faith becomes your greatest resource. It is your currency. It gives you bravery and a new, more positive perspective.

That positivity will lead you safely through the darkness of uncertainty. Without it, you'll panic and shut down. The day I got my license, that same afternoon, while riding high on adrenaline and pride, I packed a bag, and hit the road from Albany to Atlanta for the weekend. I was excited to have legal proof that I was ready to escort myself anywhere I so pleased. I was suddenly Ms. Independent.

I hopped on the highway and headed up Interstate 75 South in my shiny new Cavalier, feeling like a million bucks. I was doing pretty well, until I got closer to Atlanta. Now, if you've never been to ATL, let me paint a picture for you. Here, there are six-lane highways and the cars whiz by at approximately 85 miles per hour. And let's not forget about the fleet of 18 wheelers that are constantly commuting along this Interstate. At once, the vehicles flying by, the roar of the huge, threating trucks, aggressive drivers, and the realization that I was all alone, felt menacing.

My excitement turned into sheer horror. I was absolutely and utterly terrified! I had left my comfort zone where I was used to coasting down the small, lazy highway in Albany. Ms. Independent turned into a blubbering mess. I pulled over, called my mom and broke down crying. I told her I was afraid and didn't want to drive anymore. In hindsight, it's hilarious. That day, however, I was completely shook and traumatized.

Mom did her best to calm me. She stayed on the phone with me and talked me through it the whole way. The fear factor that nearly stopped me from moving forward, decreased, due to my mother's soothing encouragement. She assured me I could drive on the fast-paced highway safely. And you know what? She was right. I did it that day and have been doing it ever since with no fear.

I shared that story to help you see that we all feel afraid at times. Unfamiliar experiences are jolting. In our elation, we feel invincible. We imagine we can conquer the world. But when the road is intimidating and things move at a dizzying pace, our confidence wanes. If we aren't deliberate about refusing to let fear control our actions, we'll come to a screeching halt.

As you prepare to birth your vision, don't keep fear at the forefront. Put faith in the driver's seat. Break up with being scared and worried. Approach this trimester with assurance that God's hand is leading you. His feet are walking with you. He goes before you in every situation. .

Comfort zones are overrated

By now, your vision is undergoing many changes, which will become more obvious soon enough. Most women—though not all—say that, by their second trimester, morning sickness is starting to fade away. They can begin reintegrating some of their pre-pregnancy activities and start reengaging in more of what they love. Once you acclimate to carrying your vision, you will find your way back to things you once did for enjoyment before conceiving. But keep this in mind: you *will* encounter a new normal.

Your growing vision will completely change you. Life as you once knew it will become obsolete. Your decisions become less about what *you* want and more about what your *vision* needs. A reprioritization happens. You have an epiphany and realize that comfort zones are overrated. Truthfully, when you dwell in them too long, you become a prisoner. With this mindset, you welcome the stretching process, because you're ready to move into the next dimension.

Right before I began stretching myself, I had settled into a mundane routine. During my first year managing my new vision, I posted daily on social media and wrote weekly blog posts for my website. After doing it for several months, I grew comfortable with those parameters. But then, something happened to disrupt my norm. On the brink of celebrating my one-year anniversary, one Saturday morning, I stumbled across the social media page of a young man named Leon Ford. He had been unjustly shot five times by Pittsburgh police and left paralyzed when he was 19 years old. The more I researched what happened to him, I learned shocking details regarding the way he was treated by officers.

I didn't understand how, in a case of mistaken identity, Leon was facing up to 20 years in prison. He was wrongfully accused of being a gang member. I didn't get why his story wasn't broadcasted on every media outlet. Why was I just finding out about his case in August 2014 when he was shot November 11, 2012? I couldn't believe the reports I was reading. My heart ached for him, but, the more I learned about that fateful evening, I was simultaneously inspired. Leon had dealt with an astronomical amount of pain, but somehow, he was still positive. In every post I clicked on, he was encouraging others, despite what he was going through. He lost his ability to walk, but didn't lose his ability to empower. He somehow found the strength and courage to assign purpose to his pain.

I wanted to do something to help him, but I knew I couldn't assist Leon and remain confined to the small circumference of my circle of comfort. I desired to conduct an in-person interview so he could share his story with my network. That would require me branching out and breaking up with familiarity. After mental gymnastics, emotional flips, and spiritual restlessness, I decided to stretch, and break my vision out of its tiny box. On November 20, 2014, I flew to Pittsburgh and formally met Leon. By this time, I had completely abandoned my safe space and ventured out into the unknown. As you might imagine, I was nervous and nearly talked myself out of meeting him. Even though this bold move added life to my vision, I couldn't see past my fear at the beginning.

Today, I'm glad I chose vision growth over comfort zone maintenance. Our mutually beneficial connection proved both powerful and essential. After linking up with Leon, we remained in close contact. Exactly one year after learning about him, I hosted my first Gala for *The Break-Up*. He received the inaugural "Inspiration of the Year" Award, which was the start of something great for my organization. An innovative idea emerged to honor different individuals in the community every year. It is has become one of the highlights of the Gala.

Had I remained loyal to my comfort zone, I would have never gotten to know the person that sparked the launch of incredible community-focused initiative. As the event gains traction yearly, affording me the opportunity to empower greater numbers of individuals, in my mind, I always go back to first meeting Leon. This tremendous platform and opportunity to be a blessing started with that one decision to say *no* to comfort and *yes* to purpose. Since then we have become vision partners, assisting and supporting each other as we birth our God-given visions. See how breaking outside of your comfort zone can produce life-changing, positive relationships, and moments?

As you're reading, maybe this process sounds intimidating to you. You may be satisfied with your present state and don't feel ready for the changes that come along with being pregnant. That's a pretty common thought. But don't fret. The process of pregnancy isn't designed to destroy you, but rather, to develop both you and your vision. The more developed you are, the more successful and equipped you'll be for giving birth.

Adjust your mentality

As changes become more evident, you may experience a greater degree of discomfort during your pregnancy. That's because with growth comes change and with change comes discomfort. As you go through various growth spurts, check your perspective. Make sure it's positive, because how you perceive your situation can either increase or decrease the uneasiness you feel.

View the changes you're undergoing through a lens of optimism. See this as preparation for the next phase. Shift your focus from the miserable aspects of the transition to the necessity of it. When you understand why you're going through, it helps makes sense of the level of sacrifice required to get through. To clarify, if you view sacrifice from the perspective of "I can't have," you make it tougher on yourself. Try changing your viewpoint on sacrificial living. Begin saying, "I can do without," which makes giving up certain things seem less burdensome. See how that works?

Be uncomfortable now so you can be successful later. Adopting this philosophy will be helpful to you along the way. Looking at things from this vantage point will keep you from growing resentful of your new normal. Among new vision carriers, it's common to hear complaints of discomfort because they are not yet acclimated to the changes taking place. It could also be that they haven't changed their outlook from "I can't have" to "I can do without" as I just mentioned.

By now it's clear: you may as well settle in and deal with temporary discomfort—that is, if you want to grow. In the grand scheme of things, those addicted to comfort disqualify themselves from greatness. Growth inevitably invades your space and expels you from your cozy quarters of mediocrity. If your vision fits easily and snugly into the life of ease you've built for yourself, it hasn't reached its maximum potential. A growing vision cares nothing for comfortability. You can't expect to give birth to something great and remain complacent. The inconvenience of destiny must be expected, accepted and embraced. As your womb stretches it gives your vision room to enlarge.

Discomfort is a blessing

Discomfort gets a bad rap. It is viewed negatively. But in the context of being pregnant with vision, it's really positive. It is a blessing. It creates opportunities for you to reposition yourself, make new connections and walk into bigger territory. If you were never uneasy, would you be motivated to change? Of course not. The more content you are, the less likely you are to evolve. Therefore, seasons that challenge your norms fuel growth and development in you.

Your life's calling won't manifest if you're never placed in an environment that forces you to make adjustments. Anything that doesn't change is stagnant and stagnation is a deathtrap. Your unique purpose will be suffocated and sabotaged by comfort. Purpose fulfillment is impossible without pressure, pain, stretching and many of the things you'd rather not face. Your vision cannot morph into what God desires if it is limited by your addiction to bliss. Growth, enlargement and expansion will result in temporary pain, but the positive results will be lasting.

Don't you want to be unfettered, uninhibited and free to blossom? If you said yes to that, get ready for the discomfort of weight gain. During your second trimester of being pregnant with vision you will start bulging. It will suddenly dawn on those who previously paid you no mind, or were merely put off by your odd behaviors, that you are expecting. Physically, in this stage, a woman's breasts will enlarge. Her stomach will expand. With time, the entire body will transform. This transformation is necessary for the growing fetus. When you're pregnant with vision, there will be weight gain: financial weight; stressful weight; weight of partnerships; weight of new adventures; and several other weights depending on your vision. Your adaptability and ability to stretch means you can handle the blooming of your vision. You are capable of bearing up under the weight of greatness.

Some women say they feel self-conscious when gaining pregnancy weight and often become emotional about it. What they see when they look in the mirror has changed so drastically, they don't know how to accept their new state of being. Their new normal is a little *too* new and goes well beyond their threshold for change. When you become pregnant with vision, adapting isn't always easy initially. You have to accept that your greatness is restructuring you. You may find yourself becoming increasingly emotional. While these type of mood fluctuations are normal, don't let unstable emotions deter you. Your commitment to changing and growing cannot be predicated upon your feelings. Otherwise, you will be inconsistent and stunted.

We all have moments when we don't feel our very best, but that doesn't give us the right to forfeit our assignment. Take me for instance. I've never been very athletic, although I love watching sports. Growing up in a household with a father and brothers that were sports fanatics, I had no choice *but* to learn to enjoy basketball, and football. In real life, however, athleticism wasn't as much fun. As a child, I hated when the coach would select two captains and tell them to pick teams. Because I was not considered fit, I was, without fail, one of the last ones to be selected. This *always* left me feeling inadequate.

I wrestled with those feelings of being unwanted and not good enough as I grew up. Nevertheless, I was determined to fight for my vision. When the myth of inadequacy lied and said I was inferior, I shook it off. Though I was never selected to be the captain of the team in Physical Education class, I have been handpicked to be the captain of my vision. Now *I* am in control of choosing my own team. How's that for coming full circle? But what if I had let thoughts of unworthiness rule me? I would have missed out on my destiny. I would have overlooked an important fact: I wasn't chosen by man back then, but I am chosen by God right now.

And so are you. Being pregnant with vision, in all its discomforts, is a blessing. It says that God trusts you to carry something greater than you. You don't have time to get wrapped up in what others think about you. You may not be viewed as special. You might not feel great about yourself. Your blessing can, at times, feel like just the opposite. That isn't unusual for visionaries. As heavy and stressful as it can be at times, though, know this: you won't break. Burdens are often blessings in disguise. If you endure, you'll be rewarded greatly.

I can think of several moments in my life when I felt like I would break, but I didn't. When I came out on the other side, my resiliency increased. What appeared to be burdensome initially, increased my strength exponentially. It set me up to handle the blessings that came afterward. Through every hardship, God was increasing my strength and enlarging my capacity. That was the blessing in discomfort.

Here's what I want you to do. Ask yourself, *what can I gain from the discomfort that I feel?* As you think of answers, keep in mind that discomfort is purposeful. Pain doesn't disqualify you from destiny; it challenges you to push and persevere. Don't stop pressing through the pressure. Fight through the discomfort. It will make you stronger. If you wave the white flag and quit, everything stalls. If you want to see your vision work, you've got to work it. There will be no manifestation without your participation. Do something. Give it your all. Strive every day to be better and more excellent. Not better than anyone else, just the best version of yourself.

The unpleasant necessity of stretching

Ask almost any visionary and they'll get excited about the prospects of growth. Go to nearly any expectant mom and you'll see her eyes light up when her baby bump manifests. But as she continues growing, some unpleasant side effects of expansion may show up as well. Stretchmarks, for example, aren't viewed favorably. Many women complain about these visible stripes on the skin that result from the body's rapid spreading.

Putting on extra pounds *and* having blemishes can be unsettling. But the reality is, you're outgrowing things. During a natural pregnancy, your body won't fit into certain clothing or shoes at this stage. For vision-carriers, the new you will outgrow people, jobs, habits, places, and several other things. This marks the unpleasant necessity of stretching.

When you notice your transformation, don't try to stuff yourself into places, relationships and predicaments that can no longer accommodate your needs. Branch out. If you keep on engaging in the same activities, hanging with the same people and doing the same things, while carrying a heavier load, you will be increasingly overwhelmed, and uncomfortable. It is impossible to experience increase if everything around you has a lesser capacity than your vision requires. You can't pour a gallon of water into an 8 ounce glass, can you? You need a container large enough to hold that amount of liquid. As your vision enlarges, think bigger. Just like the pregnant woman knows when her jeans are too small, know when your circle, mentality, and environments are too small.

Take a moment to ponder a couple of questions: *can you identify people and things in our life you have outgrown during your pregnancy process? Are you suffocating by still trying to cram yourself into these scenarios and situations that no longer fit?* If so, break up with this bad habit. Wave goodbye to the familiar. Sticking with what you know may seem best to you right now, but it isn't necessarily best for you. Don't be afraid to trade the commonplace for the uncommon places. Growth and comfort rarely coexist. Optimal growth means maximum discomfort. As you feel the weight of change, welcome it. Initially, the heaviness will seem like too much. It's not. God built you to carry this seed.

Whether you know it or not, stretchmarks prove this point. I'll explain more so you can appreciate the things that you may view as a nuisance. What I find most interesting about stretchmarks is that, they don't just appear on the belly. They sometimes show up on a woman's, buttocks, legs, back and arms. They result from the skin tearing during pregnancy due to rapid growth.

A visionary's stretchmarks are a lot like natural stretch marks, in that, leaders are stretched in more than one way—not just in the area of their vision directly. You may be simultaneously stretched in multiple ways: emotionally, financially, physically, socially, intellectually, and spiritually. The stretching may extend into your relationships and career also. But no worries; stretchmarks remind you that you have adapted to the weight of the load. If you couldn't stretch, you would break.

Think about a rubber band. When it's sitting in a container, it seems small. But if you pick it up, wrap it around two fingers and pull the band in opposite directions, what happens? It stretches. You can observe in real time that the piece of elastic is much larger and stronger than it originally appeared to be. Through trials and tribulations, God increases your elasticity. He makes you more flexible and highly adaptable to change. If you never tug on elastic, you remain ignorant of its potential. If the vision never grew inside you, you would remain ignorant of your ability to stretch far beyond what you knew to be possible. Your stretchmarks are reminders that your capacity has increased and you survived what could have broken, or utterly destroyed you.

In the beginning of my journey, I didn't have any metaphorical stretchmarks. There were no growth indicators present. I lacked outward signs that I could do it. I was living my life un-stretched, with my potential untapped, just like an unused rubber band. Being placed in circumstances that pulled me in new directions expanded my abilities and revealed my capabilities. With each test I passed and each storm I survived, I realized more and more, *I can handle this!* There's nothing like pressure and adversity to show you the truth of who you are. Nowadays, I see stretchmarks everywhere.

Once upon a time, I wasn't too happy about the difference I was noticing. It didn't feel good when my finances were stretched and I had to change my budget to accommodate my growing vision. But the stretchmarks appeared and I was able to manage my money. I was discouraged when I outgrew some relationships. But again, I developed stretchmarks, which got me through the heaviness of lonely moments. I felt like I was completely out of my element when God called me to a higher realm of faith. Nothing about my circumstances aligned with my vision. Fear wanted to grip me. But stretchmarks appeared and with every adversity, my faith increased. The more I embraced my growth, the more I appreciated my stretchmarks.

I was being stretched but I didn't break. Did things get tough? Absolutely! But God literally increased my capacity. As I began to develop an appreciation for my metaphorical stretchmarks, then I began learning very valuable lessons concerning my process. I realized I was not limited to the parameters that I was accustomed to functioning in. I had been given the aptitude to go beyond what was familiar to me. As your vision grows, embrace all that comes along with it—the good, the bad and the ugly. Everything about your process is necessary.

There's more than what meets the eye

While growth on the outside is becoming more visible during the second trimester, what's taking place on the inside is of great significance, too. What pregnancy looks like outwardly doesn't compare to what's taking place internally. There's more than meets the eye. It is interesting how we assume that, what we perceive externally is an accurate reflection of internal progress. But it isn't. What rises to the surface is only a glimpse of what is beneath the surface. That's why it's never good to completely judge a process by what you can perceive. It's often the things you *cannot* see that make the greatest impact.

So then, what exactly *is* going on inside the woman's belly during the second trimester? The body parts that began developing in the first trimester, like eyes, ears, fingers and toes, are now starting to gain some function. The fetus is moving more: twisting, turning, kicking and punching. The heartbeat is getting stronger. The brain and lungs are developing so the baby can survive independently after delivery. At this phase, the fetus depends on the mother for everything while it is in development. Similarly, in the beginning stages of your vision, you may depend on others to help you grow, but you won't always have them to depend on. At the proper time, you will be able to live independently. Be sure that, while you are in your co-dependent season, you develop your vision so that when the time is right, it will be self-sufficient.

In this trimester, the reproductive organs of the fetus are also developed, allowing the gender to be revealed. Remarkably, even with all the new developments, the unborn fetus is still relatively small, reaching about two pounds by the end of the sixth month. What you are able to see at this point is limited. There is no way you can, with the naked eye, witness the complex processes and great progress taking place. This is why judging by what you see is futile. Again, there is more than meets the eye.

During the second trimester of your vision, there will be increased momentum and function. Your innovative thoughts and ideas will become physical manifestations. You will have greater clarity of purpose. Most importantly, you will begin to notice growth and movement. The movement may initially startle you, just as it does an expectant mother when she feels the first flutters of her fetus. But soon, you will be accustomed to the movement and progress of your vision.

Premature birth

Initially, I was a little apprehensive about writing about the premature birth of vision. But then I started thinking. We all face detours, hardships and derailments at some point. Therefore, it is absolutely necessary to write about it. The more I mulled it over in my head, I asked myself key questions: what happens if someone is reading this book and they feel as if they have birthed their vision prematurely? How will *Pregnant with Vision* help them? How will this book assist those who are carrying vision for the first time? What about the person who is experiencing complications? How will this book speak to them?

As I pondered this more intensely, it became abundantly clear that skipping over premature birth would be a disservice to you, my reader. So, I started doing a little research and discovered that, according to the Centers for Disease Control and Prevention, 1 in every 10 babies are born premature. Carrying the fetus full-term is ideal, but it's not always possible due to complications. Of course you always hope and pray for the best, but sometimes your journey requires that you endure adversities. It's a very tough reality. And if you're anything like me, you would prefer to ride down easy street. However, when you've been tasked with something great, it's not always that simple.

Some of the greatest things in life are birthed through adversity. You must learn to forsake your plans and embrace the plans of the Creator. Although it may be difficult, remain faithful to the process. When carrying vision, things will not always go as planned. You might go into early labor. While it is my prayer that you have a healthy pregnancy and delivery, I understand that each path is distinctive.

In my research, I also found that, even if a woman does everything right, she can still deliver early. When I read that, I imagined that, someone, somewhere, must be wracking his or her brain, trying to figure out what went wrong. They are asking, *what could I have done differently?* Perhaps you are one of those mindful, careful, detail-oriented people that made the effort do everything right. Nevertheless, you still experienced complications.

You must not allow yourself to be terrorized by guilt. Don't blame yourself for what has happened. Giving birth prematurely doesn't mean that your vision will not survive, nor does this unfortunate occurrence diminish its value. Even when a second-trimester birth happens, and the child is underdeveloped, its value isn't lessened. Doctors and nurses still do everything they can to help the premature baby survive. They understand its worth. You must view your vision the same way. It may be underdeveloped, but it's still valuable. It may not make you any money just yet, but it's still valuable. It may require all of your time and effort, with little to no returns, but it's still valuable.

It's normal to want everything to be perfect. It's typical to desire that all the components of your vision be fully developed before you expose it to the world. We all desire a complication-free process. But there are seasons when our plans don't pan out the way we hoped and expected. This is a good time for you to do some soul-searching. How should you respond if the reality doesn't live up to your expectations? Will you allow this disappointment to make you give up on your premature vision, or will you create a nourishing environment to contribute to its growth and development? Be flexible. You never know what life will bring. But, whatever comes, God has prepared you in advance to handle it.

Incubate your vision

Just as a premature baby spends a significant amount of time in the neonatal intensive care unit (NICU), likewise, your vision may need to be incubated while it fully develops. During this critical period, you will need to monitor your vision closely, making sure it has everything it needs to become strong and independent.

Incubating a premature vision protects it during its critical state. It is not yet ready to be revealed or exposed. Rather than rushing to show it off, spend some time alone with it. Be attentive. Shut out distractions. When a premature baby is born, sometimes, parents aren't able to hold the infant right away. The baby may not even be allowed to have many visitors because of its fragility. Visitation could put the baby at greater risk for further complications.

If a series of circumstances led to the premature birth of your vision, go into protective mode. Incubate and insulate it. Too many opinions, ideas and hands around a premature vision puts the fragile endeavor at greater risk. Incubation makes it stronger and it develops it daily. Soon your vision will be strong enough to survive independently and be ready for the big reveal.

Before we advance to chapter 5, know that the lessons and principles shared here in chapter 4 will serve you well throughout the entirety of your pregnancy. As you head into the more advanced stages, you will be forced, over and over again, to stretch, adapt and adjust to change. So be flexible, remain passionate, and above all, be open to the process. Let's continue on the journey.

5 You're getting closer

As you inch toward your due date, prepare to be stretched, challenged and pushed outside of your comfort zone even more. What's to come will be so worth it.

It's funny. When people see me, they actually say *"Hey, it's The Break-Up!"* I've grown accustomed to that greeting and I welcome it. I understand that it's not about me; it's about my vision. We've already talked about the time when my vision wasn't visible, so I'm grateful it is now impacting lives. A while ago, no one knew what was in me. These days, I can't seem to hide it. The more I surrendered to my process, the more God grew *The Break-Up*, and continues to grow it today.

Your vision will grow as well. Just keep going. Enthusiastically approach your third trimester by focusing on all the possibilities of your future. This optimism will help you through challenging times, of which there will be plenty. But let nothing stop you. Your life is about to be dramatically altered. Everything will revolve around your vision as you inch closer toward giving birth. Before you're able to push that baby out, however, there are several different symptoms of pregnancy you're likely to experience first.

Though largely unpleasant, you can handle them. On days

when you feel like you can't, remember that you're so close. Soon, you will reap the big rewards of enduring such a long and strenuous process. In the course of waiting, don't dare allow the demands of being pregnant with vision to make you think the load is too much. You have been designed to bring forth destiny. Furthermore, relief is coming and it's coming sooner than later.

Prepare for pain, restlessness and pressure

If you don't like change and growing pains, uh-oh. You won't like your third trimester—at all. The most important thing that will occur during this final stage is growth. By now, you already understand that growth is constant. Therefore, change is constant. Needless to say, we can't discuss growth without discussing change.

During the last trimester, the woman's body evolves along with the unborn baby. Typically, her stomach swells nearly three times its regular size. The baby goes from weighing about two pounds, to anywhere between six and nine pounds during the last trimester alone. That's *a lot* of growth! The protruding belly, which becomes the woman's largest body part, is now heavier, causing her greater discomfort. The larger the belly grows, the more tiredness and achiness she feels. As the fetus gets bigger, her symptoms become stronger. As a visionary, your increasing pain and fatigue is an indication that you're closer; the birthing process is near.

You can expect to lose more sleep the closer you get to delivering. During a natural pregnancy, slumber becomes more difficult to come by because of the circumference of the mother's belly. Finding a relaxing, comfortable position when lying down can be next to impossible. As your vision continues to grow, you will have to reposition yourself. This will increase comfort somewhat, but not totally. No adjustments of any kind will fully alleviate the pain and restlessness. But it can lessen it. You'll find that, at this stage, what was once soothing, can actually cause misery. That's because you've outgrown what you were accustomed to for so long. Don't be afraid to move differently, change your stance, adjust your pace, or reposition yourself to accommodate your growing dream.

Even when expectant moms do what is most feasible in terms of positioning, they still lose sleep because they're constantly waking up to use the bathroom. The pressure on a woman's uterus during this phase is enormous. The closer she gets to the end, it increases that much more, making pressure one of the most unpleasant, difficult-to-manage, change indicators. Growth introduces new challenges and creates no shortage of frustrating moments. As a visionary, keep this in mind when you experience pressure buildup: it's a signal that what you have been hoping, praying and believing for is on the way. You may toss and turn, get aggravated and vexed, but hang in there. The emotional rollercoaster is to be expected because there is so much going on.

Making moves

Parts of your vision that seemed stagnant and undetectable in the earliest stages, will change significantly at this stage. Your vision is outgrowing its comfort zone and preparing for birth. The movement taking place inside, will become far more evident on the outside during the final trimester. Remember in the beginning when the fetus was just getting used to being in the womb? It was too tiny to perceive. That is no longer true at this juncture. The fetus becomes less comfortable and more active. It is positioning for birth, while continually growing and moving. Your vision will reflect this behavior as well. You will see things you've been working so hard on start to take shape. Momentum will increase.

The flurry of movement and activity will contribute to your restlessness, but don't let that worry or bother you too much. Power players, movers and shakers are always on the go. Sometimes, their vision requires them to rise earlier and go to bed later than everyone else. While others are sleeping, they are making moves. Visionaries have seasons of insomnia and this is not to be viewed negatively. Here's why. Once you give birth, your vision is just like a newborn baby requiring feedings, changings, and lots of tender, loving, care. It will be totally dependent upon you. Therefore, the restlessness you're currently experiencing is serving as preparation for what's ahead.

Imagine a pregnant woman never having any sleep challenges. Adjusting to getting up throughout the night to take care of her precious bundle of joy, would be incredibly challenging. If you never had to burn the midnight oil before giving birth, you wouldn't be able to handle the level of responsibility, work, and sacrifice that is required after delivery. God is strategic in all things. He never unleashes inexperienced visionaries. He uses pregnancy and all its difficulties to prepare you for the birth of your unborn vision. Embrace each experience and be mindful of its significance.

Manage your weight

In the beginning of your pregnancy, gaining weight was encouraged. It was necessary for proper growth and development. In your present state, although new responsibilities increase weight, proper management of it, is of utmost importance. Gaining an excessive amount of weight during your pregnancy can cause various harmful side effects and jeopardize the health of your vision. Complications like gestational diabetes, where your body does not produce enough insulin, can result from poor weight management during a natural pregnancy.

Just because weight is inevitable doesn't mean you shouldn't keep it in check. With any endeavor comes stress and more tasks to accomplish, but the management of stress and responsibilities is critical. Eat what nourishes you. Take on what enriches you. With natural pregnancy, the unborn baby consumes whatever you consume. This holds true when you're pregnant with vision. Consumption should be limited to what is healthy, necessary and beneficial, because not all weight is healthy weight.

In light of this truth, you can easily see why everything and everyone can't be a part of your pregnancy. You can't take everyone's advice. You can't internalize negative talk and energy. Devour the wrong thing and it will devour you. Consume the wrong thing and it will consume you. If you open yourself up to the wrong thing, it will swallow you whole. Feast on positivity and encouragement. Choose a nutrient-rich diet that your vision can feed off of with positive results. If anything has potential to be harmful to your vision, remove it from your metaphorical diet.

Before I understood this, when I was pregnant with *The Break-Up, LLC,* for a time, I was carrying way too much. I was gaining unnecessary weight that took its toll. I was taking on the responsibilities of others, all while trying to carry my own vision. I didn't know how adversely the weight of someone else's vision could affect mine. Shouldering everyone else's burdens can cause you to wrongly believe that *your* vision is too heavy. Truth is, you need to drop theirs and focus on yours. You have to opt out of carrying others' vision during your pregnancy—and after birth—not because you don't believe in theirs, but simply because it's too much for you to handle.

When you're overly-invested in someone else's vision, it can cause you to become overwhelmed. It all gets to be too cumbersome. Once I started experiencing the side effects of unnecessary weight gain, I had to be honest about what I could and could not take on. I needed boundaries. I didn't have enough respect for my limitations. Even knowing this didn't make the choice to lose some of the weight easier. I wanted to lug it all around, but I didn't have the strength. I didn't want to disappoint the ones I desired to help, but I needed to be truthful and realistic with them, as well as myself.

If you find yourself needing to drop the weight of someone else's vision, you will soon discover who cares for your vision, and who is selfishly motivated. People who care will encourage you to get rid of unnecessary weight, so that you can birth a healthy vision. They will want you to avoid the potential damage of overloading and overburdening yourself.

Being bogged down doesn't only occur when you try to nourish someone else's dream at the expense of your own. Taking the wrong advice has a similar effect. Over the course of my life, there have been those who meant well, but their advice wasn't beneficial to my process. I encountered people that had unfavorable experiences in their past. They were still living with the guilt, disappointment and bitterness, so what they had to say came from a negative place.

In your efforts to manage your weight in the third trimester, don't allow others to inflict the weight of their past experiences on your present opportunity. Even some people that may genuinely love you, want to help you, and desire to see you win, are covered in the residue of negative history. Therefore, it seeps into their pores and oozes out through their advice. Just because you value their opinion, doesn't mean you have to apply it to your situation. Be wise. Be prayerful. Be careful. Filter the information. Stop accepting everything from everybody. It will cost you your vision if you don't get a grip. You must be selective.

Negative motivators

I wasn't selective enough at first, plain and simple. I was constantly eating words of negativity. There were some who said *it will never work*, or *I should have gone to medical school*. Others didn't say much, but fed me their negative energy. I was literally surrounded by negative motivators. That sounds oxymoronic, right?

What is a negative motivator? It is a person that is aware of the value of what you are carrying, but they still try to steer you away from destiny. They attempt to motivate you to go in the opposite direction of your dream. They tell you to abort your vision for any number of reasons: you aren't ready; you don't have enough money; you don't know enough; somebody like you isn't cut out for that. They basically tell you to quit. Walk away. They give you theories about why your path is unwise and will result in failure. Be mindful of negative motivators. Some of them are unintentional dream-crushers. Even though they mean no harm, that doesn't mean they are harmless. They are, in fact, unhealthy for your pregnancy. They are toxic to your vision. They constantly spew opinions, criticisms and advice rooted in doubt, fear and anxiety.

No wonder the weight I was picking up wasn't healthy weight! I was letting negative motivators feed me junk food with zero nutrients. What was I thinking? My vision suffered temporarily, but I made some changes. I got away from negative motivators. I grew closer to God so I could hear Him more. I became more selective about the advice I received and accepted. You have to do the same thing. Develop such a great love for your vision that you will do whatever is necessary to protect it. Don't allow anything to jeopardize it. Strengthen your bond with your vision and you will literally fall in love with what God has planted within. That attachment will cause you to make changes and sacrifices you never imagined making before. You'll work to pick up weight when you need to, and drop it if you have to.

Like me, you will have to take a few steps back and purge your metaphorical diet to properly manage the weight of your vision. This action step will require you to make tough decisions. As your load gets heavier, you will need to be more disciplined. Weed certain people out of your dream garden so they don't ruin the seed growing there. Your weed-whacking phase may lead you to cut out those you love most, because they add on too much unhealthy weight. It hurts when you get a revelation that friends, relatives and acquaintances you thought would always be there are negative motivators. Once you see it, painful or not, you must do something about it.

Don't let loyalty to toxic relationships kill your vision. You've gotten too far into your pregnancy for you to jeopardize the health of your unborn vision. Evaluate your diet. Make the necessary changes. Don't say you value your vision if you are unwilling to make any sacrifices for it. What are you prepared to give up? Are you willing to walk away from negative motivators? Are you serious about only accepting the best advice? Are you prepared to drop dead weight, even it offends someone you love and respect? Doing what is necessary may not feel good now, but you'll see the worth of it all when you finally birth your healthy vision.

Keep going

I come from a large family: seven brothers and six sisters. As a child, on Saturdays, mom would wash and press all the girls' hair. One at a time, she would wash our hair, put big plaits in it, and move on to the next child. First, Shavette; second, Dianna; third, Shante'; and lastly, me.

On one particular occasion, when it was my turn to get my hair pressed, I was sitting on the kitchen floor playing with Popsicle sticks. Yes, Popsicle sticks. I used to collect them when I was a little girl. My mom said, "Quinny, go put your Popsicle sticks away and come back down, and get your hair pressed."

I replied, "Yes ma'am," and made my way upstairs. For some reason, still unbeknownst to me, when I got up there, I decided I wasn't going to stow away the Popsicle sticks as I was told. Instead, in my six-year-old brain, it made more sense to sneak them back downstairs. So I came up with my ingenious plan. I put the Popsicle sticks in my shirt, tucked the shirt into my pants and then bolted down the stairs. Mind you, the sticks were clicking together. How could I not know that was a dead giveaway? I looked like a real-life episode of "America's Dumbest Criminals." I still laugh at myself about this.

"Did you put those sticks up like I told you?" my mother

asked when I reentered the kitchen. Without flinching, I replied, "Yes ma'am." Yes, I really thought I could get away with it. Don't judge me.

"Don't lie to me," Mom rebutted. But in true Quinte' fashion, I stuck with my doomed-from-the-beginning plan right to the bitter end.

"Mommy, I *did*," I repeated my fib with the most credible expression I could feign.

Needless to say, my mother was not fooled. I got a nice, old-fashioned, Alabama whooping for being dishonest. On top of that, the incriminating evidence, my dear collection of Popsicle sticks, came tumbling out of my shirt. I looked like a full-blown idiot. I was caught red-handed. Mom made me throw every single stick away. I was so hurt. I can still feel the sting of that punishment now. It taught me a good lesson, however, about doing things right the first time around. Had I obeyed, who knows? I might still have those Popsicle sticks and one less beating for the books. But my defiant nature got the best of me.

Throughout my childhood, there were many times I got into trouble for failing to submit to authority. Even in adulthood, though I have earned college degrees, most of my training comes from the school of hard knocks. I'm one of the people that needs to learn stuff the hard way. I challenge norms, push boundaries, and march to my own beat … sometimes. You see, defiance is not *always* an option.

There is no way around some processes, like the process of giving birth. We don't get to skip ahead, be exempted from challenges, or cheat the system. By the time you enter your third and final trimester of pregnancy, you know this full well.

You have accepted what's to come. You realize you will suffer. You know pain is inevitable. Discomfort is a part of it. You will feel depleted a lot of the time. Yet, you are submitted to this process, because it's the only way to give birth to your vision. You recognize that you will experience fatigue on the homestretch. Still, you dig deeper. You are aware that you have it in you. You have the wherewithal to continue going, despite the ups and downs physically and emotionally.

That doesn't mean you don't have internal anxiety. At this point, you may feel a mixture of excitement and anxiousness. These mixed emotions are common near the end. You may also feel an overwhelming sense of uncertainty, as if you are unprepared for what's ahead. Though you are committed to seeing this through to the end, the plethora of emotions can still cause you to question if you're truly ready. You are. Trust that you will finish strong. The process has prepared you for the birth of your vision.

Even though you can't see every detail, you must remain optimistic about the outcome. As months have gone by, the lengthiness of the process has gotten to you on occasion. Sometimes, the slow passage of time can cause discouragement. You get worn down. This, too, is typical.

Don't allow time to distract you, though. Utilize it to prepare you. Focusing too much on the wait will demotivate you. You'll disengage and sink into a slump. Redirect your focus. Realize that every day, week, and month that goes by is serving to develop you. You just have to stick it out. God hasn't brought you this far for you to give up right before you step into manifestation.

Rest

You're over being pregnant. I get it. You feel like you've reached your threshold and at any moment you're going to break. The good news is that, the breaking points at the end of your process are actually beneficial to the unborn vision. Breaking points are really just moments that bring you closer to giving birth.

Consider what it means when the mother's water breaks. The baby doesn't always come right away, but the mother-to-be *is* a step closer to welcoming her child. When you reach your breaking point, you're *really* close to the end, too. The blessing is the result of the breaking. When you get here, you can't rely on your strength alone. You've done all you can physically do, and it may not be quite time to birth your vision. So, what do you do?

When you've run out of energy and ideas, the best thing you can do is rest and let the process work. If you *don't* rest at the appropriate time, then you'll become busy but unproductive. Your busyness doesn't guarantee growth. Productivity is a byproduct of the right strategy, timing, and persistence—not busyness.

It's easy to confuse being busy with being productive, because being productive *causes* you to be busy. However, the two are not synonymous. Did you know that resting is also a form of productivity? Resting doesn't mean you are unmotivated or uninvolved. It gives you time to restore, replenish, reflect and renew. This can enhance your workflow. Rest and reflect on how much your vision has grown throughout your pregnancy.

If you're rushing through life, not taking time out to rest and recharge mentally, physically, spiritually and emotionally you can't grow your vision to its full potential. The lack of rest could be disastrous at this stage in the process. This jogs my memory and takes me back to an evening when I was with a good friend. She was hosting her husbands 30th birthday party. The theme was "The Roaring 20's" and we got dressed up in our pearls, fascinators and fishnet stockings. We had ourselves a good ol' time.

Near the end of the party, I figured I'd gather my things and head home. When I left, most everyone was still up dancing and having a great time. There were about 15 steps I had to walk down before getting outside. I had on six-inch heels and my keys in my hand. Hurriedly, I made my way down the stairs. Because I didn't take my time, the heel of one of my shoes got caught and *boom-pow-thud-crash!* I tumbled.

No one could hear me or see me, because everyone was still upstairs enjoying themselves. When I reached the bottom of the staircase, I was facedown. My dress was up around my waist. One of my shoes was hanging by the strap around my ankle, but my foot had slipped completely out of the shoe. Do you have the visual yet? The worst part was, my car key punctured the palm of my hand. Talk about painful. Sheesh! It was *really* painful.

After I injured my hand *and* broke my shoe, I realized I should have been more careful, deliberate and patient with my steps. As the saying goes, hindsight is 20/20. That realization came too late and I paid the price. I was rushing for no reason, which is something we all have done at one time or another. But when it comes to your vision, a hard fall can be damaging.

In the third trimester, as you're waddling around, you have to maintain your balance, avoid rushing unnecessarily, as not to harm you or your vison. Resting in God will help you slow down. Settle yourself. Get quiet. Hear His voice. Let your mind travel back to the beginning. Assess the milestones and accomplishments worth celebrating. This can serve as the greatest encouragement.

It's already in you

I had the opportunity to honor the owner of E.F.F.C.T Fitness during the 2017 Anniversary Gala. I selected *"Dooley"* to be a recipient of the 2017 Award of Inspiration. He started his fitness center in his two car garage and since then, has outgrown three locations. I am amazed at how he continues to grow and change the lives of so many individuals. During the interview I asked Dooley "what advice would he give entrepreneurs or individuals who have not yet pursued what they've been called to do?" His response was *"Everything that you need is already inside of you. Stop overthinking it, stop looking to everyone else, it's inside of you."* Those words stuck with me.

If only we all would possess such great confidence that everything we need to give birth to our vision is inside of us. We wouldn't get weary and discouraged quite as easily while waiting for the arrival of our birthing season. All you need to complete your life's assignment is *in* you. In order to tap into it, you have to focus less on what's *around* you. You see, if God placed everything you needed around you, you would neglect what's inside you. Activating your purpose requires that you reach within. To be clear, your purpose isn't what you do, but it's who you are. Once you activate who you are, then the things you do will automatically align with your purpose. When you grasp this concept, you won't have to ask yourself, *what is my purpose?* The question will change and become, *what should I do to activate and develop my purpose?*

You don't have to look for your purpose outside of who God created you to be. Spend less time stressing over what you feel you are lacking. Do not consume yourself with the things that you don't have. God will provide what you need when you need it. Concentrate on this truth: all that is necessary for you to seize this moment and do what you're called to do, is in your possession.

The treasure is inside. It's in there. Stop despairing without cause. Stop believing you need more than you already have. Don't get ahead of the process. When you obsess over what you think is missing, you forget to show gratitude for, and put to use, what is presently there. Redirect your thoughts. Don't peer at the deficit. See the opportunity to receive more blessings instead. If you are in need of something or someone to help you to fulfill your purpose, God will make sure the void is filled. Whatever you don't have, you don't really need yet. When the fullness of time comes, you'll have it.. You have been created with greatness, for greatness.

The Process Is Preparing You

In December 2016, I felt led to launch "10 Days of being a Blessing"—a kindness campaign on behalf of *The Break-Up, LLC.* Though I am usually private about good deeds, I opened it up to the public to encourage others to join in. I was pleasantly surprised by how many people were inspired to participate in performing random acts of kindness. The goal of the initiative was to break up with being selfish, so we could be a blessing and make someone smile during the Christmas season.

On the first day of the challenge, I went to lunch at a local Atlanta restaurant called *Roasters* with a co-worker named Kim. While there, I met a server named Denise and felt moved to bless her. I remember she had such a positive attitude to go along with her beautiful smile and pretty dimples. Something about her warm spirit let me know she was the person I was supposed to sow into that day. I wasn't sure why, but I felt it in my heart.

Through my acts of kindness, something wonderful transpired. My friend Kim decided that *she* also wanted to be a blessing. Together, we were able to tip Denise 100% of the tab, which we found out came in handy. Our kind server told us she was working two jobs and was trying to get into grad school. She was so grateful! It felt good to bless this young lady. I know what it's like to work in a restaurant, trying to make ends meet. Remember I told you that I worked my way through college as a waitress at Longhorn? That made the moment extra special.

It also caused me to reflect on the fact that everything we do is preparing us for our future. I didn't know while waitressing, that I would become pregnant with a vision someday. I wasn't aware back then, that the challenges I faced, were developing the character necessary to walk in my purpose. God knew it, though. He had been setting things in order for years. He has been doing that in your life as well.

Even when you weren't aware of what was taking place in your life, you were being prepared through every test that you would face in your future. You didn't see the significance of the process then, because it's difficult to see the big picture when adversity is right in your face. When you're walking through a blanket of darkness, you can barely make out anything. But if you don't abandon the process, night eventually turns into day. If you stay committed to the process you will receive clarity. You'll discover that the tough times were preparing you for purpose all along.

You were born with so much potential, and because you've made a conscience decision to utilize it, it has matured into purpose over time. The maturing stage wasn't easy, but you managed to get through every tragedy, broken heart, failed relationship, death of a loved one, rejection, fear, insecurity, pain, failure and so much more. You didn't allow what challenged you to hinder you. You didn't let what negatively provoked you, prevent you from living a purpose-driven life. That's why you made it here. The circumstances that should have broken you, were used to build you up. Your pain was necessary because it matured you for the birthing process.

If you never endured the pain of the pregnancy, birthing the vision would destroy you. Every setback was beneficial, because it taught you how to be patient. Waiting renews strength. Rejection was helpful, because it eliminated people and things that weren't intended for your destination. Every time you pushed through adversity, you were pushing yourself deeper into your purpose. Nothing you have endured was in vain; it was all used to mature your potential into purpose. You went through a period where you were carrying around greatness and didn't even know it.

Thankfully, during that time, in your ignorance, you didn't self-sabotage. Think about all of the wrong turns you took, mistakes, and poor decisions you made. When you didn't see your worth or understand the value of your vision, there was something in you that wouldn't let you give up. Something deep inside of you knew that one day, a light bulb would pop on. You would have an epiphany and finally see your value. Before we discover the worth of our vision, we don't treat it well. Notice I said "we," because I'm guilty, too! Thank God for grace. He knew we would eventually change our entire lifestyle. Even before the transformation happened, God was preparing us all along.

Let's Reflect

I understand that your process has been exhausting and you've given up a lot to get here. As I told you earlier, reflecting is a great way to encourage yourself, so let's do that before moving on to the next chapter.

You had to break up with some people and things you once couldn't imagine life without. You may have left close family and friends behind. You lost money and sleep. But of all the things you lost, your faith wasn't one of them. This process activated it. Now, your faith is greater.

It has allowed you to see beyond your circumstances, leave behind what is familiar, and take a chance on something greater. You survived that phase where you didn't see any growth. You clung to your belief in the super early stages when you felt like you were just feeding your imagination. You still nurtured your vision as if you would see benefits immediately. No one around you knew you were pregnant. You were too embarrassed and afraid to reveal it. You were overlooked, mistreated and ultimately, counted out. You have been talked about, doubted and frowned upon. You even second-guessed yourself sometimes, but you stuck with it. Let's reflect a little more.

You didn't abort your unborn vision. You could have opted out, but you placed your hope in the creator. You depended on Him to give you strength. You understood that it wasn't anything you could do on your own; you needed Him. You made up in your mind that you were going to go through with the pregnancy, no matter how afraid you were. Whether or not you had the support of family and friends, you refused to terminate the pregnancy. Your vision is now so close to being birthed and you're still growing.

Right now, I know it's uncomfortable. You have come through a lot. You're ready to see manifestation. Have a little more patience. You're almost there, but your vision will not be delivered until it is ready. During this final stage, exercise your faith, which has been tried in the fire of affliction. It will sustain you until the day you hold your soon-to-be-birthed vision in your arms. When you consider what you have survived, let it fuel your faith even more. You are prepared for what's ahead. You are well on your way to birthing a healthy vision. Now let's continue moving forward.

6 Symptoms of a Growing Vision

Don't allow the symptoms of the process to deter you from completing the process.

Pressure During the Process

My parents are old school. My father was born in 1935, so you know I'm not kidding when I say they're old school. I remember as a kid, during the summer, my dad loved grilling. Everyone knows that my dad cooks the best ribs. Before he put them on the grill, he would have my mother cook them in the pressure cooker first, to make sure they were tender. See, I told you my parents are old school; I don't even know if they sell pressure cookers anymore. Nonetheless, my mom would put the ribs inside and close the lid tight. As they began to cook, the pressure would build up in the pot. Once the maximum pressure the pot could hold was reached, the steam would come shooing out. This was a sign that what was inside the pot was ready to come out. When you're pregnant with vision, you will experience pressure when it's time to birth it.

Pressure occurs when what's growing on the inside of you no longer has enough room to continue to grow. When I refer to pressure, I'm not just referring to physical pressure on the body, but also emotional and mental pressure. The closer you get to the birth of your vision, you will feel it. As a baby grows inside a woman's womb, she begins to experience pressure. During pregnancy, pressure is common in the joints, pelvis and lower abdominal area. This typically happens because the uterus is stretching so that it can securely house the baby until time for delivery. This pressure increases as the due date approaches, because the baby is preparing for its exit. By this time, the baby has outgrown its developing space inside its mother's womb and the increased pressure is a sure sign that birth is very near.

As it relates to your vision, you will feel increased pressure as you reach the end of your pregnancy. Some of the feelings you initially felt when you first found out you were pregnant may resurface. It's normal to wonder if you can handle all that comes along with your vision. Remember in the beginning you didn't know if you had what it took to endure all that came along with pregnancy? Now that you're experiencing more pressure, you find yourself asking the same questions. *Will I have all the support I need? Am I really ready for this? Will I be good at this? How will I juggle being a visionary along with everything else I am to others and myself?* The growth of your vision is causing pressure to build up and you're becoming more uncomfortable in your current state. Although pressure is expected, don't overly consume yourself with the concerns you have; it just means you're getting closer to birthing your vision. Pressure helps to create an awareness regarding what is taking place on the inside of you. It is designed to make you mindful, but not stress you. It simply prepares you for what you are getting ready to produce. Ask any mother, and she will probably tell you that when the pressure began to become unbearable, she knew it was time to make sure her birthing plan was in place, along with all the immediate essentials her new baby would need, because it was only a matter of time before the baby was born.

So, when you feel the pressure of your vision building up, you must consider your priorities and your resources. Deal with what is necessary and rely on trusted sources to assist you with the rest. No matter what, don't allow the pressure of your growing vision to discourage you from completing your process. All of the greatness inside of you can't stay inside of you, so the pressure is just letting you know that greatness is soon-to-be released. Greatness trapped inside of you is nothing more than wasted purpose. Don't allow pressure to break you prematurely, but let it serve as preparation for the delivery.

When the pressure becomes too much for you to carry, then you will birth your vision. Pressure may slow you down, but never allow it to stop you. You are equipped to endure whatever lies ahead as a new visionary. You won't necessarily get it right all the time, but you will eventually find your rhythm and learn how to best nurture and grow your vision, while still being great at everything you already were.

Swelling

Have you ever paid attention to a pregnant woman's ankles? Usually, near the end they are enlarged twice the size, causing increased discomfort. The discomfort may even cause the expecting mother to not fit into shoes she bought specifically for her pregnancy. As a visionary, you will experience metaphorical swelling, also. You will know you have entered this phase when you are not able to find comfort in the very things you once needed for the process. The discomfort of the swelling will shift you out of what was once your comfort zone, so that you can endure the remainder of the process, even if that means you do nothing but rest.

Swelling is an extremely common side effect experienced throughout the pregnancy process, more common in the third trimester. There are many factors that can cause one to swell during the final stage. One of the major causes is lack of rest. Some women remain extremely active throughout their pregnancy and keep up with routine activities and responsibilities for as long as possible. In fact, some women push themselves too hard, when the weight of the unborn baby requires that they slow down and relax. Slowing down and relaxing is essential during the final phase, because the body is preparing for the birthing process. The same holds true for vision. There will come a time when you have to slow down and relax. Too much activity during the final stages will take a toll on you. The weight of your unborn vision is too valuable for you to bear weight of unnecessary things. The more swelling that occurs, the more uncomfortable the expecting mother becomes. Swelling makes it difficult for one to complete daily activities or to fit clothes, shoes, wedding bands and other items. The expecting mother must acknowledge the indicators that signify she needs rest. The same holds true with vision. There will be indicators which will notify you that you need rest. Taking on too much as you near the end of your pregnancy will cause metaphorical swelling for you, and the reality of how you feel will only cause further discomfort. Sometimes, it's necessary that we push past how we feel, but there comes a time when you must use wisdom and acknowledge when you've reached your threshold. I find it common amongst visionaries that they don't like being still. However, the still moments of the process usually bring the most clarity regarding what should be done next. When you ignore the indicators to rest, you cause unnecessary pain and hardship. On the contrary, when you rest at the appropriate time, you put yourself in a better position to give birth to a healthy vision. Optimal productivity is a sign of adequate rest. During the final trimester, your threshold reduces and you may have to decrease your activity so that your vision remains healthy. Once you notice swelling, you must be willing to relax, rest and trust the process.

7 The Process Is Preparing You

Don't become so consumed with birthing the vision that you fail to maximize the process required to develop the vision.

In the final trimester, the unborn baby is preparing to breakup with the womb. Breakup? I know that sounds harsh, but remember, breaking up isn't always easy, but it's often necessary. Without breaking up with the womb, the baby wouldn't survive. Isn't it amazing that the very thing that helped you to live could be the very thing that kills you if you don't let go at the appropriate time?

Comfort zones can become vision-killers if you don't get your vision out in time. Just like the woman's belly becomes too condensed for the baby to continue to grow and thrive, your comfort zone can literally suffocate your vision. Your vision cannot live inside of you forever. Your metaphoric womb was needed for protection, nourishment, and growth, but when your vision has reached a certain point, you must release it. Therefore, breaking up is needed in order for life to occur. You cannot allow your fear of being broken to cause you to kill your healthy vision. Remember, some of our greatest accomplishments are a result of brokenness. The thing that breaks you has a way of pushing you at the same time.

Have you ever had your heart broken? It felt like you would never get over it, right? But do you ever just sit back and acknowledge that the heartbreak somehow made you better? The thing that once caused you to feel like you couldn't make it another day somehow became the driving force behind you fulfilling your purpose. Everything that breaks you isn't meant to destroy you. Too many people stop living life at the point they were broken. Is that you? Did you stop living when the relationship ended? When the loved one died? When you lost the job? When they told you that you couldn't do it? Did you prematurely abort the process because of what broke you, or did you allow it to fuel you? For those of you who are undergoing a season of breaking, don't allow it to make you give up. Instead, let it push you into the next dimension of greatness.

Your process isn't over just yet; you've come too far to end it right here. And if you have stopped at the breaking, I challenge you to change your perspective of brokenness. If you haven't given birth to greatness, that just means it is still in you.

The relationship with your metaphoric womb will only be beneficial to your vision for a specific period of time. As the baby moves closer to the delivery day, it will begin breathing, swallowing, and sucking while it's still inside of the womb. The baby is literally preparing to leave its comfort zone by developing essential characteristics for survival. These characteristics are vital components of living a healthy life. Your vision will also begin to develop characteristics for survival, which indicates that the time is near to share your vision with the world. Some of the characteristics include originality, substance and influence, just to name a few. As your vision develops these characteristics for survival, others will be impacted by its growth. I can recall when I discovered that my vision started developing survival characteristics. August 30, 2014, I celebrated The Break-Up, LLC's one-year anniversary. I invited supporters of The Break-Up to help me celebrate, but the night took a positive turn that I'll never forget. Different individuals began sharing with me how they were inspired by my vision -- how my innovative approach helped them to get through depression and helped them to break unhealthy cycles to become the best version of themselves. I realized at that moment that although my vision was still growing inside of me, it was developing the characteristics required to survive outside of me.

A place for your purpose

The unborn baby is also doing a lot of moving in a very tight space during this stage, because it is repositioning for birth. The baby will completely flip upside down, causing the head to be positioned in the pelvis area. No wonder you're experiencing so much pressure these days. The position of the baby is extremely important during the birthing process. Essentially, what's happening in this stage is the baby is preparing for birth.

Towards the end of the pregnancy, some women will experience pain in their pelvis area. This is definitely a sign that the birthing process is near. In most cases, at around 36 weeks, the baby moves down into the brim of the pelvis, and when this happens, the body releases hormones which actually soften the ligaments, allowing more room for the unborn baby as it positions for birth. Oftentimes, this causes both pain and unwanted pressure for the expecting mother, but it also creates a larger opening for the unborn baby to get through.

When I relate this process to our vision, I get extremely excited, because it lets me know that there is room for your vision and room for mine, as well. Your vision may resemble someone else's vision, the market for your vision seems to be overly saturated and you're thinking to yourself, *how will my vision thrive in this market? How can I get to the next level?* The good news is that there is room for your vision.

What God has placed inside of you is unique and it's purposeful. There are people out there that need your vision specifically. I hear so many people talk about how they waited too late or that too many people are doing what they love, and they don't want to seem like a follower. Remember that your purpose can never be duplicated. Therefore, your vision is a byproduct of what the Creator has placed inside of you. Even with all of the other amazing visions in the world, your vision is needed. It will be successful and it will change lives. God has a specific assignment for your vision and He will provide you with opportunities for your vision to be a blessing. Just like the hormones are released to soften the ligaments of the pelvis so that the baby can get through, God will release things on your behalf and soften the hearts of those that have resources, so that your vision can get through. You must have faith that God has made room for what it is He has called you to do. There is a scripture found in Proverbs 18:6 that says, *"A man's gift makes room for him, and brings him before great men."* The vision you're getting ready to birth is going to make room for you and it will bring you before other great people. Know that what is inside of you is great and it is getting ready to be released to the world. The way has already been made; continue on with the process so that you can give birth.

Preparation

Preparation, preparation, preparation! Pregnancy prepares both you and your vision for birth. Lack of preparation can cause complications that will lead to the incubation of your vision. It's so easy to get caught up with thinking about the birthing process, that the excitement of introducing your vision to the world can sometimes make you want to fast forward the process. However, you must be careful not to become so consumed with birthing your vision that you fail to maximize the preparation process. It is the sacrifice needed for the reward. Without going through the preparation, the birthing process could end up being detrimental to your vision.

Can you think of a time in your life where you had to go through unnecessary pain because you rushed the process? We get excited when we hear the term "birth," because we think of giving life. While this is true, we must consider the associated factors. Birth is also synonymous to trauma, meaning there is a great level of distress that both the visionary and the vision will undergo before life is granted. It has been said that when a woman gives birth, she comes extremely close to death. Isn't it interesting that bringing forth life has the potential to kill you?

Therefore, preparation is necessary in order to survive the birth of your vision. The mother has to push the baby out of her womb and you, too, will have to push your vision out of you. There is no easy way to be pushed. Being pushed implies being forced, and sometimes you will have to force some things out of you in order to give birth.

When you understand the value of what you are giving birth to, your only option is to push. You have pushed your entire pregnancy - past fear, past insecurities, past those who doubted you. But the final push will be proof that you were prepared for the birthing process.

During the final trimester of your vision, you can expect to feel discomfort as your vision has outgrown its comfort zone, and it is time for it to be impactful to the world. As your vision gets into the birthing position, you may feel unsettled due to the final movements and changing before birth. The movement of your vision can cause you to feel a plethora of emotions, similar to the ones you experienced when you first discovered you were pregnant with vision. These emotions are normal, as you are preparing to undergo trauma.

You've been growing and changing throughout this entire process and its all been extremely purposeful, even if you haven't been able to see or appreciate its value. It's common that we don't see value or significance in the beginning. A perfect example is one of the most common symptoms shared amongst all women, which is the increase in breast size. As the woman goes through the process, it is natural for the breast to increase significantly in size throughout the pregnancy. Initially, it just seems like you're gaining weight because of your increased appetite and the growing baby. While this is true, there is greater significance in the woman's growth. The woman's breasts are gearing up for the most important job for the survival of the baby, which is to provide nourishment.

Growth is necessary, because it increases the mother's capacity to produce what is needed for the survival of the baby. It's so amazing how the woman's body naturally creates exactly what the baby needs so that it can continue to grow healthy and strong even after birth.

When I examine the correspondence of our vision to the natural pregnancy process, it helps me to understand how growth increases our capacity to provide our vision with what it needs to survive. Therefore, we don't have to consume ourselves with the how, because God has already given us what we need to be successful.

Your capacity to nourish your vision is inherited throughout your process. This is why the process is necessary; rushing through the process will cause you to forfeit vital components that are needed for the survival of your vision. During the actual pregnancy process, the woman does not see the milk in her breasts, but when it's time to feed the baby, the milk is there. Let that soak in for a moment - what is needed for the survival of the baby is there even when it is intangible. You won't always see the resources for your vision, but know that it's already there. Just as it isn't necessary for the mother to worry how she will feed her baby, it isn't necessary for you to worry how you will feed your vision.

The woman had breasts before the process, but the process provides her with the milk. You were born with purpose before you were ever pregnant with the vision. But the process of growing your vision is what provides you with everything you need. So, forfeiting the process will cause you to lack, but when you go through the process, God will provide you with what you need. It's so easy to become frustrated when what you need isn't in front of you. If you're not careful, you will consume yourself with worrying about what's already on the way.

I can recall numerous times during my own process when I found myself worrying about how things were going to turn out. But looking back, all the things I worried about worked out during the process, even when it seemed untimely.

Perhaps there is a mother reading this and your milk didn't produce the very first day, or not even the second day. The good news is that babies aren't born with nutritional needs for the first couple of days after being birthed, because colostrum has all your baby needs. Colostrum is the secretion before the actual milk is produced. The colostrum is all the baby really needs during its first few days after birth to supply its nutritional needs. This means your baby won't starve, and by the time your baby works up an appetite, your body will produce the milk. There will definitely be tight moments when you feel like your vision is lacking, but you must trust that during this phase, even when it doesn't look like it's going to work out, it will.

Your vision will not go without what it needs in order to survive. Just because things don't happen in the time we expect doesn't mean that they aren't going to happen. Trusting the timing of the process is just as important as trusting the overall process.

Now that you have a greater understanding for the pregnancy process and why it is essential for the growth and the development of your vision, keep in mind that the process is also essential for the visionary. Both you and your vision are simultaneously preparing for birth.

We all experience stretching, changes, and pain, but there is no need to worry, because you'll be prepared for it when the time comes. Even in the natural pregnancy process, the woman will begin to experience birth-like symptoms before the actual time of the birthing process. Remember that everyone has a different process and not all symptoms are the same, but you must trust that your process has prepared you for what you're giving birth to.

Braxton Hicks contractions are very common in the final trimester. I like to call these practice contractions. These practice contractions can last for several seconds at a time, but they eventually stop. The discomfort and the intensity of the pain may cause the expecting mother to feel like she's going into labor. Some women find themselves at the hospital, only to find out that it isn't time yet. Practice contractions are an indication that the birthing process is near. Although the pains of labor are more frequent and more intense, Braxton Hicks contractions still help to prepare the expecting mother for the real thing.

In the final trimester of your vision, you will experience discomfort, and the intensity of your stress level and/or anxiety may increase, leading you to believe it's time to give birth to your vision, but not just yet. The discomfort you are experiencing is just preparing you for what's ahead in the delivery process. The discomfort is the most common symptom with preparation. By now, you know that change is uncomfortable, but, again, I will tell you that it's completely worth it. It's imperative that you, as the visionary, are prepared for what's coming.

God will sometimes allow uncomfortable and unfavorable things to occur in your life in order to prepare you for what you're giving birth to. Preparation is not intended to make you fearful or stressed, but it is simply to make you ready for what lies ahead. It increases your capacity to handle the hardships of the process. As you come to the final moments of your process, trust that everything happening in this season is only preparing you for what will take place in the next season. Preparation isn't intended to destroy you, neither is it intended to intimidate you, but it is to strengthen you. The magnitude of your vision requires that you are strong enough to handle all that comes along with it. You must have faith that what is being utilized to prepare you will not separate you from your vision, but bring you closer. Sometimes, pain and discomfort makes us feel that we're moving further away from what is intended for us, but it actually brings you closer because it makes you stronger.

Can you imagine birthing a vision without a process? The vision could potentially destroy you, because you would have something in your possession that you weren't prepared for. This is why it is so imperative to completely embrace the process and all of its discomforts, because it's almost time for you to give birth to the greatness that's inside of you.

Remember, you were chosen for this. No one else can birth your vision for you; therefore, you must continue with the process until it is complete. The birth of your vision requires preparation. Don't give up now; you're almost there!

Final Stages of the Process

You have officially reached the final stage of the process. Both you and your vision have endured a strenuous process of growth and development. What was once a tiny seed of potential is now a fully developed purposeful vision. Though it may not be time for you to deliver your vision just yet, you are now considered full term and your vision has the ability to survive if you birthed it before the expected due date. During a natural pregnancy, a woman can deliver her baby at 37 weeks and it would still be considered full term, even though, by standard, there is another three weeks before the woman reaches the end of pregnancy. At 37 weeks, the unborn baby is still growing, but it has the essential components to survive outside of the mother's womb.

Ideally, you want to wait until your vision is completely ready before you birth it, but in life we don't always encounter perfect conditions. Sometimes, we experience unexpected occurrences that alter our idea of the process. These unexpected occurrences may not always seem perfect, but it is important that you trust the entire process.

It's easy to become worried and frustrated when we encounter unexpected things throughout the process of birthing our vision. I wish I could say to you with assurance that you will give birth naturally and that the process will be easy, but I can't. You can do everything by the book, yet still encounter bumps in the road. There is no such thing as a perfect process, but there is a such thing as a necessary process.

There are times when what is necessary doesn't always coincide with what we imagined. Just like the physician will determine what is best for the mother and the baby, God will determine what is best for you and your vision. God will allow different things to occur during the process, not because it's favorable, but because it is necessary.

In the natural birthing process, some women will undergo a cesarean in order to birth the baby. A cesarean is often formed to ensure the safety of both the mother and the baby. Although this process is different from what is considered the natural birthing process, it still results in the birth of the baby. A Cesarean is an invasive surgical procedure performed on the woman's stomach and uterus in order to deliver the baby. The common named used to describe this procedure is known as a C-section. Not all cesareans are planned. There are some instances where unforeseen circumstances occur and an emergency c-section is necessary for the survival of the baby. Cesareans reduce the level of trauma for the unborn baby. Remember we talked about being pushed and how traumatic a push can be? Sometimes, there isn't enough time for the mother to push, or maybe the baby isn't in the right position. Or, perhaps the women's cervix didn't open up enough to push the baby out, or the overall process would be too strenuous for the baby and the mother. Sometimes, it has nothing to do with the mother and everything to do with the baby, or vice versa. These are just some cases where a cesarean is often the best process for birthing the baby. The good news is the way that the baby is delivered doesn't reduce the value of the mother, the baby or the value of the process. In fact, a cesarean further validates the value of the baby. The doctors understand what is at risk of being damaged or lost, so they go through a major surgical procedure to remove the baby.

Your vision may also have to undergo a cesarean. The value of what you are carrying is too great to jeopardize its survival. There is someone that needs you to birth your vision by any means necessary. Perhaps you've endured a long process and things just don't seem to be working out the way you planned. Maybe you're at the verge of giving up on your unborn vision. It is in these moments when God sees the value of what he has placed inside of you, and he sometimes has to take out what he has placed in you so that you or your vision isn't harmed. He knows that the trauma of the natural birthing process could potentially harm your vision, so, instead, he takes it out before the process can destroy it. Sometimes, we have to be cut so that our vision can be released. If you find yourself going through something painful right when you're at the verge of delivering your vision, maybe it's God's symbolic way of surgically removing your vision so that he can get it out of you before the process destroys it. God also knows what we are able to handle; he knows when you're at your breaking point and, in such cases, he will rearrange your process so that you aren't destroyed by it. I've had to endure a metaphorical c-section while carrying my vision. I found myself drowning in a relationship that was unhealthy for me. One day, it abruptly ended and I didn't understand. I now understand it was God's way of cutting me so that my vision wouldn't die in the relationship. If the relationship hadn't ended, I would not have birthed my vision. It would have died inside of me. But because God understood the value of what I was carrying, he altered my process to save my vision. Initially, I was upset because I had witnessed others go through a process without being cut. However, over time, I realized that their process also came along with its discomfort, pain and detours.

8 The Pressure Is Positioning You

The pressure from the process creates a pathway for your vision to push through.

Don't compare your birthing process to the birthing process of someone else, because you don't know all of the components of their vision. The components of each process are tailor-made for both the vision and visionary. I say all the time as it relates to social media, *you can see their posts, but you don't know their story.* What you face during your birthing process is necessary for what you are carrying.

If your vision doesn't require special accommodation, that doesn't mean your gift is invaluable; it just means that your process requires something different. Every vision has a unique process; although, some components of the process may be very similar to the process of another. Don't become consumed with someone else's process. When you compare your process to someone else's, you end up desiring something that could have the potential to be more harmful than helpful to your vision. What was needed to save someone else's vision has the potential to destroy yours, so don't allow the progress of others to prematurely push you to a place that your vision isn't prepared for. You don't know all of the details of their process and vision, so stay focused on your process.

Your vision may require a longer process than others. For those mothers who make it to the ninth month of pregnancy, fetal activity changes over time. What was once aggressive kicks become more condensed movements, due to the lack of room in the belly for the baby to move around freely. The final stage of pregnancy is relatively restrictive for the baby as the mother reaches her maximum capacity to support its growth.

The comfort zone has been completely disrupted as a result of positive changes and growth. As the baby outgrows its comfort zone, it is preparing to exit the womb. Stop trying to find ways to regain comfort in places you've outgrown; instead, prepare yourself and your vision for birth. Preparation isn't designed to cater to your comfort, but it's designed to coincide with your needs. What you need and what feels good won't always be parallel. Sometimes, the things that feel the worst are the things we need the most.

I'm reminded of growing up as a "PK" (Preachers kid), I was in church all of the time; All day Sunday, Tuesday for bible study, Thursday for choir rehearsal, Friday for pastoral night and Saturday to clean up for Sunday. I just didn't understand why I needed to be in church nearly every day of the week. One time, I got caught reading a *Goosebumps* book in church. I put it inside my bible so that it would look like I was involved. That didn't last. I got caught and was forced to interact in the actual church service. I still laugh at myself. Now that I'm older, I understand that being in church as frequently as I was taught me about service. My service to God has taught me how to serve people. It all coincides with my purpose. Sure, I wanted to be outside riding my bike with my friends, but the preparation for my vision required something different, even though I didn't understand it at the time. The most uncomfortable situations often prepare you for what's ahead. Discomfort can definitely leave you feeling overwhelmed and frustrated, but you must remember that it's temporary and you are now closer than you've ever been to birthing your vision.

When you can't find comfort in your circumstances, you can find peace in knowing that it won't last forever. Most mothers define the final month as being the most uncomfortable, due to constant growth with limited space, which leads to physical stress on the body. Has your vision outgrown the parameters of your womb? If so, prepare yourself for the arrival of your vision.

Earlier in the book, we talked about pelvic discomfort caused by the repositioning of the baby. As the baby positions itself in the birthing canal, it causes pressure in the mother's lower back and pelvis area. The weight and the repositioning of the baby make it difficult for the mother to find comfort during her final stages. The undesirable pressure is necessary though, because it allows the pelvis area to open up. If the pelvic area remains closed, then the baby cannot be birthed vaginally. It is here that we understand the significance of pressure.

The weight and the pressure combined are responsible for

creating an opening that is needed for the birth of the baby. As the baby adds pressure to the pelvis, it opens wider over a period of time, eventually opening up the cervix wide enough for the baby to get through during birth. The opening of the cervix is known as dilation. In the beginning stages of the pregnancy, it was necessary for the pelvic area to remain closed for the security of the baby, but at the appropriate time, pressure is applied to create an opening. Premature pressure can cause a premature birth. Some women experience their cervix opening prematurely and, as a result, they become bed-ridden during their pregnancy, in efforts to release the pressure that would cause the cervix to fully dilate.

As it relates to your vision, you have to be mindful not to allow others to prematurely pressure you into birthing your vision before it is time. There will be those around you who believe in your vision, but they don't understand all of the components of your process. Although they mean well, you must not allow the added pressure to send you into premature labor. Sometimes, you will need to go on metaphoric bed rest to release yourself of the pressure caused by the process of carrying your vision. Pressure doesn't always have a negative connotation; it can be a positive attribute when the timing is right.

We often get discouraged when we feel increased pressure, but it is actually what creates a pathway for your vision. Increased pressure from your vision means that a door is getting ready to open in your favor and your vision will soon serve as a gift to the world. This feeling may be a little strange, because you've grown accustomed to some doors being closed; however, your vision will create opportunities for you that you weren't eligible for initially.

Don't become so comfortable with rejection that you fail to recognize opportunity. You must not grow discouraged when you don't have access to certain doors. Your lack of access isn't always a permanent no; sometimes it just means not yet. If the cervix is opened too soon, then the baby will be delivered prematurely, which could lead to further complications. God understands how some opportunities may be harmful to your vision, so he makes some things inaccessible to protect your vision. The further you get in your process, the more grateful you'll become for all the times God said no. I've learned that every *no* will better prepare you for your life changing *yes*.

Expectation

Now that you're feeling the increased pressure of your growing vision, you know that, at any time, you could go into labor. I like to think of this phase as the expectation phase. You're now expecting to birth your vision any day. You may even become restless, finding yourself double-checking to make sure everything is perfect for the birth of your vision. In the natural pregnancy this phase is known as nesting. While the restlessness you feel is completely normal, trust that the process has prepared you for the arrival of your vision. It is important that you keep your stress level down during this time. In a physical pregnancy, the stress of the mother has a direct effect on the baby. The same is true for your vision. When your stress levels are high, it greatly affects the health of your vision. One of the most common causes of elevated stress levels during the final month of pregnancy is wondering when the baby will arrive. The expecting mother starts to experience a variety of symptoms: Stomach dropping, leaky breasts, stronger Braxton Hicks contractions, extreme fatigue, difficulty breathing, swelling, and the list goes on. The extreme discomfort is a sure indication that delivery day is near. You may be experiencing your own delivery-day indicators and you may find yourself stressing more. It is imperative that you properly manage stress during this final stage. Your body is sending signals to let you know that the time is coming soon, but, ultimately, you have to wait for when the time is right.

The thing about *soon* is that it has no definitive date. It's not long, but the question still remains, *how long? Soon* can leave you both excited and frustrated, but it should never leave you feeling stressed. *Soon* is proof that you've gone through a process that has placed you in the mindset of expectation. *Soon* means that all of the pain and discomfort you've endured will be replaced with a greater reward. Don't grow discouraged when soon seems to be taking longer than you expected. Remember, your vision isn't birthed in your timing, but in God's perfect timing. *Soon* creates an anxiousness that may cause you to find ways to catalyze the remainder of your process. It's common for expecting mothers to try at-home remedies that serve as a catalyst to speed up the labor process. You know how it is when your patience grows shorter and you reach a point where you feel desperate.

The discomfort that the expecting mother is feeling seems like it's too much. I remember when my sisters were pregnant; they would go walking around the park in hopes of going into labor. Walking is believed to assist the baby with making its way into the pelvic cavity so that pressure is applied and, of course, the more pressure, the greater the opportunity.

Another common self-induced mechanism is taking Castor Oil. This yucky substance causes stimulation of the bowels and uterus causing contractions.

I remember when my niece Ayanna was pregnant; during her last month, she would take castor oil to try to induce labor. Her contractions would increase for a moment, but, still, no baby. No matter what she did, my sweet little nephew didn't come until he was ready.

We can try to speed up the process, but the fact remains that we have to wait until the time is right to birth our vision. Trying to manipulate the timing of the birthing process can lead to further discomfort. You never know why *soon* is taking longer than you expected. No matter how ready you feel, you have to trust the process. Don't try to jump ahead of the process. Jumping ahead of the process will cause your vision to suffer. We could save ourselves a lot of stress and pain if we would embrace the process instead of rushing it. Don't let your emotions get the best of you; continue to trust the process.

False Labor

You may think it's finally time to birth your vision. You're experiencing all of the symptoms that indicate your vision can no longer stay inside of you. By now, you have everything set and you're ready for the physical manifestation of your vision. You feel the pressure and the contractions of your vision getting stronger, and you feel confident that it's time to birth your vision. Unfortunately, sometimes, before you experience real labor, you may experience false labor.

It is extremely common for the expecting mother to feel the pressure of the baby and intense contractions, but still not be in real labor. There are women who go all the way to the hospital, just to be told it isn't time yet. The Doctor understands that false labor can resemble real labor, but it takes the real labor to deliver the baby. The Doctor lets the expecting mother know that the contractions aren't strong enough and the pressure is not great enough to deliver the baby, so the mother is sent back home. Can you imagine how frustrating it must be to experience pain and pressure, but still be sent back home because it isn't time yet?

I'm reminded of a story my mother shared with me. She said when she was in labor with me, she went to the hospital twice before she went into real labor, and she was sent back home both times. She shared that the pain was intense, but the doctor insisted it wasn't time yet. My mom said she was so disappointed, because she really felt like she was in labor; her false labor felt like the real thing, so she thought. When she got back home for the second time, the pain grew more intense, but she just sat there and endured it as long as she could, because she didn't want to get back to the hospital only to be turned back around.

Her false labor symptoms frustrated her to the point of her not wanting to go back to the hospital, but she said there's something about real labor that pushes you. The pressure became too great and the contractions were too strong for her to sit at home any longer, so she woke my dad up and they went back to the hospital for the third time. When she arrived, the doctor confirmed that she was in *real* labor.

When she told me the story, I couldn't help but reflect on my own personal experiences of being in false labor with my vision. I have felt like I was ready for something, but it just wasn't time. I've cried, pouted, and complained, but God knew that it wasn't my time. Each time, I would go to him expressing my concerns of labor, he turned me around, notifying me that what I was experiencing was only false labor. Have you ever felt like you were truly ready for something, and God said *not yet?* Sometimes, the pain and the pressure of the process are so great until we go to God and we *tell him* that it's time. And, just like the doctor, God says the pressure isn't great enough and the pain isn't strong enough, and he sends us back to finish out the process. I experienced being sent back to finish the process with writing this book. I made a couple of social media announcements, planned and prepared for the book release. I was certain that I was in labor and ready to give birth to my vision. Just when I felt like I was in labor, I was in an automobile accident that slowed me down. I broke several bones in my right hand. And, yes, I'm right-handed. The injuries resulted in surgery and an extensive healing process to regain mobility. The process was also very expensive, causing me to have to use money that I delegated to my vision to take care of myself. Talk about being frustrated! I didn't understand what was going on. I endured the process, and I was experiencing the pressure and pain of labor, only to find out it was false labor. It wasn't my time to deliver my vision and, although I wanted everything to go as planned, I had to go back into the process until it was time for me to give birth. This has been one of the most frustrating things I've experienced throughout my entire process. Thankfully, God isn't pressured by our emotions and he makes us wait until the time is right. False labor symptoms are just gearing you up for the real thing.

Don't get discouraged when you are turned around; instead, use it as the final moments of preparation, because when it's time for real labor, there is no turning back. Although false labor can be intense, it isn't as intense as real labor. Eventually, the contractions will stop with false labor if you change your position or walk around, but this isn't the case with real labor. When you're really in labor, the pain continuously increases and the contractions intensify. Like my mom said, you feel a push. The push you feel will let you know that the baby is getting ready to come. The same will occur for your vision. You will feel a push that is undeniable. You won't be able to rest and the pressure will not subside as you change activity. Nothing else will matter other than giving birth to your vision. This time, when you go to God, he will let you know it's time and you're ready to give birth to the vision you've been carrying inside of you for quite some time.

9 It's Time To Birth Your Vision

You must push past the pain of your process to give life to your vision.

Real Labor

Finally, you're really in labor, and it's time for you to get ready to bring your vision into the world. You will soon experience the joy of birthing your vision. The pain and the pressure you feel when you really discover that you're in labor may override the excitement you thought you would feel. That's normal; we all get distracted by pain and pressure sometimes.

Experiencing something extremely painful can make you lose focus on your vision, but only temporarily. Pain is a part of birth, and even if you opt to take something to help you manage the pain, you will still experience pain during some parts of the process. Along with the pain, you may feel a little scared and worried, and you may even wish you could retract some time, due to the severity of the pressure you feel. No matter how unprepared you feel, there is no turning back when you're in labor. In the natural labor process, the mother must dilate ten centimeters before she can give birth vaginally. The dilating cervix is what creates a pathway for the baby.

As it relates to your vision, things will start to open up for you.

Your pain is creating a pathway for your vision to make its grand entrance into the world. Every painful experience in your life will be used to make room for your vision. Don't forfeit the process because of pain; remember that your pain has purpose. Dilating can take a while, but no matter how long it takes, your vision is coming forth. Your vision cannot stay inside of you forever; it has to come out. You will feel the undeniable pressure and it may be a bit overwhelming, but your vision is making its way down the birthing canal. You've endured the process of pregnancy, now you must endure the labor pains.

Labor pains

As the labor process progresses, the pain you feel will intensify. The pressure will be undeniable and you will feel the urge to push even though it may not be time to push just yet. When a woman first goes into labor and her cervix isn't completely dilated, the doctor will instruct her not to push. Pushing up against a cervix that isn't completely dilated can delay the delivery process if swelling occurs, which makes it more difficult for the baby to get out. We equate labor to pushing, and although that's a part of it, it isn't the totality of labor. Before you can push, you have to endure the pain of the contractions and the pressure. There is no need to exert all of your energy pushing on a closed door, because you will need your energy for when God opens it up for you.

Pushing prematurely can lead to a prolonged process. When you're in labor, there will be people around you encouraging you to push. We've all heard the saying, *when it gets tough, you have to push yourself.* While this saying is absolutely true, we must remember that timing is a valid factor, as well. There will come a time when you have to sit and endure the pain; in these moments, pushing is not necessary. Notice I said *endure the pain* and *not wallow in the pain.* Enduring pain comes with an expectation that it will end. Wallowing in the pain comes with a mentality of permanence. The pain isn't permanent; therefore you must endure it. You can't always push yourself out of pain immediately, because it is through pain that you will be prepared for the delivery of your vision.

When an expecting mother pushes prematurely during the delivery process, she exerts unnecessary energy that she will need once the cervix is completely dilated. The same goes for your vision. Stop pushing on doors that God hasn't unlocked yet. Pushing on a locked door will only cause you to waste the energy you will need to actually walk through the door once it's been unlocked. Pushing prematurely can cause undesirable delays. Just like swelling can occur in the woman's cervix, making it more difficult for the baby to get through, we can block out a window of opportunity by arriving too early. Don't allow the circumstances of your process to cause you to get in your own way. Pushing with a purpose is more beneficial than pushing because of pain. This is why it is important to have people around you who are knowledgeable and understand the complexity of birthing your vision. They won't push you before it's time or beyond your capacity. Instead, they will coach you at the necessary rate to help make your process as smooth as possible. There are moments in the process when you will need encouragement to push, but there are moments in the process where you will need wisdom to know that it isn't time to push yet. The doctor will instruct the expecting mother when to push, because he understands the significance of pushing at the appropriate time.

There is no doubt about it, labor is downright hard and painful. You will reach a point of exhaustion and you may feel that you can't get through it. When the pain and pressure build up to the max, it will be time for you to push. No wonder most women have someone in the delivery room with them, to coach them throughout the process. God understands how difficult labor is; therefore, he will assign people to you to help you birth your vision. I like to refer to these individuals as vision partners. Your vision partners will encourage you when you feel like you have given everything you've got. They will remind you that you still have something in you that must come out. They will encourage you to rest when it's necessary, and they will encourage you to push when it's necessary. They will go through the birthing process with you.

Although labor is difficult and intense, some may encounter a period of time where the process slows down and the contractions aren't coming as fast and as strong as they once were. There are several factors that may cause labor to slow down. Usually, when this happens during the natural process, the doctor will administer some form of medication to get those contractions rolling again.

Remember, contractions are what open up the cervix so the

baby can get through. In the process of birthing your vision, you may also feel your labor process slowing down. Initially, things will seem to be progressing and moving along, but then things slow down. Although you know you are at the brink of birthing your vision, it seems like your process isn't going as planned. That's when God will step in and provide you with something that will speed up your labor process. Just like the physician understands that the labor process is time-sensitive, God also knows your process is also time-sensitive and he will see to it that you deliver your vision. God will sometimes cause something to intensify your process, bringing more pain and more pressure.

When your process is intensified, it isn't to destroy you or your vision, but it's actually an assistance mechanism. When we have grown accustomed to the pain, we stop pushing; we think we've figured out the process, so we slow down on the intensity. That's when something will show up and act as a catalyst to the process. Sometimes, it feels like blow after blow. I know it feels like it's always something and, perhaps, it is; but just know that it's necessary. Often, when we get really close to birthing something really amazing, we need assistance. This doesn't mean you or your vision isn't prepared, but it does mean that it is valuable. Your vision is too valuable for God not to provide the necessary assistance for you to birth it.

Get In Position to Push

The baby is in position, your cervix is dilated, the pressure is intense, and the pain is severe. Now, it's time for you to get in position to give birth. Your position is key to birthing your vision, and pushing can be ineffective if you're not in the right position. It's the combination of your position and the push that delivers your vision. Once you reach the pushing stage of labor, that means you have entered into the transitional phase. Once you are fully dilated and contractions are constant and close, you are approaching the moment you've been waiting for all of this time - delivery. By this time in your labor process, you may feel exhausted and overwhelmed. You just want it to be over and you're more ready than ever to see your vision. Don't allow the pain you feel in this moment to distract you. Stay focused; you're getting ready to push out your vision.

PUSH

Finally, it's time for you to push with the pressure and the pain. Your window of opportunity has opened and it's up to you push so you can birth your vision. The urge to push will become overwhelming as the pressure builds up, and your vision can't stay in much longer. A close friend of mine allowed me to be in the room while she was giving birth to her son. It was amazing to see a life enter into the world. I was fascinated by the entire process. I remember the pushing phase most vividly. When it was time for my dear friend to push, she didn't care what she looked like or what anyone in the room was thinking. She was focused and ready to see her baby. The pressure and the pain had intensified so until she wanted nothing more than to deliver her son. Her labor process provided me with essential components for pushing out vision.

When it's time for you to push out your vision, it is important that you are not distracted by external factors. You can't be concerned about how you look and what everyone is thinking when it's time to give birth to your vision. You have to zone in and focus all of your energy on pushing. Your desire to give birth must also match the intensity of the labor process. Pushing requires that you dig deep within yourself. As you push your vision out, you will find that you have been equipped with strength that you didn't know you had. You're stronger than you ever imagined, but you won't find out until you push. Don't let the pressure intimidate you; zone in and push. Some women can't effectively push without the pressure.

Therefore, the pressure is necessary to increase the impact of the push. Hence, pain, pressure, positioning, and pushing all produces purpose. Every component of the process is necessary for you to deliver your vision. At this point, you have to give it all you've got. No more holding back, no more being conservative. Don't worry about how you look or sound, just push. There is nothing pretty about pushing, and you might have to cry, scream, and vomit all while you're pushing. Right now is the time for you to dig deeper than you've ever had before to get this vision out of you. Some will deliver faster than others, but you will deliver, even if you have to be cut.

I talked to a couple of my sisters who had to have an episiotomy, which is a surgical cut that is necessary when you are fully dilated, but not unable to stretch enough to get the baby out. An episiotomy is done to prevent tearing. Although episiotomies are no longer very common, there are cases when they are necessary. Tearing causes more damage than cutting. Therefore, it's better for the physician to cut you with precision, rather than allowing you to tear incorrectly. For some, you will have to have a metaphoric episiotomy so that you can birth your vision. God is not going to allow your vision to tear you apart, therefore he will metaphorically cut you with great precision if necessary.

If you have reached the point of full dilation, pushing with pain and pressure, but your vision is still inside of you, expect to endure a season of cutting. Just like some women undergo a C-section, some will undergo an episiotomy; either way, the cutting is necessary. As discussed previously, cutting is not always done to harm you, but to help you. God knows the value of what he has placed inside of you, so even if it means cutting you to get it out of you, he will.

Have you experienced rejection during your labor process? Perhaps, that's God's way of cutting you. Have you reached a financial deficit? Perhaps, that's God's way of cutting you. Has a valuable relationship ended? Whatever type of surgical incision you receive during labor will be unique to your vision. However, keep in mind that the cutting is only to preserve the greatness you will soon give birth to. Remember earlier in the book when we talked about cesareans? We learned that God will do whatever is necessary to save your vision. Due to the rarity of an episiotomy, you just might have to labor a little longer until your vision is birthed.

Let your contractions build up, breath, and you know what's next? PUSH!

The more you push, the closer you will be to birthing your vision. As you begin to push, you will see your vision peeping out. Some mothers see the crown of the head with each push, but she has to push hard enough to get the entire head out. Do you see the crown of your vision? Keep pushing; it's almost out. Don't you dare get frustrated and give up. Your vision needs you more now than ever before. You have to push. I know you're exhausted and you're in great pain, but you're almost there. Somehow, you will find the strength to keep pushing; your vision partners will be there to coach you along the way, and God is standing there overseeing the entire process. PUSH!

The head has finally made its way out, and with just a few more pushes, your vision will be tangible. Dig deep; you're almost there. PUSH! And just when you felt like you didn't have anything else left, congratulations -- you have given birth to your vision!

On your last push, God was standing right there pulling the greatness out of you, and he has cleaned off the residue of the process so you can see the greatness that has been harvesting inside of you all along.

As I write these final words, I am extremely emotional, as my pregnancy process has been very difficult. I've grown, stretched, made mistakes, wanted to give up, lost sleep, lost loved ones, cried, screamed, pushed, and I have finally given birth to my vision.

I am so grateful that I didn't give up prematurely. I'm so grateful that I trusted God through this process and now I get to hold my vision in my hand and nurture it so that it blesses the entire world.

I broke up with carrying greatness inside of me, and now I have the opportunity to deliver greatness to everyone I come in contact with.

It's your turn to deliver your vision to the world. Congratulations on birthing your vision. You are now a visionary, and it's time for you to change the world with your God-given vision.